Two Yellow Butterflies

CAROLINE MALONE

BALBOA.PRESS
A DIVISION OF HAY HOUSE

Balboa Press books may be ordered through booksellers or by contacting:

Balboa Press
A Division of Hay House
1663 Liberty Drive
Bloomington, IN 47403
www.balboapress.co.uk
UK TFN: 0800 0148647 (Toll Free inside the UK)
UK Local: 02036 956325 (+44 20 3695 6325 from outside the UK)

Print information available on the last page.

ISBN: 978-1-9822-8192-2 (sc)
ISBN: 978-1-9822-8194-6 (hc)
ISBN: 978-1-9822-8193-9 (e)

Balboa Press rev. date: 08/06/2020

For Mum, Reet with eternal love Dink x

CONTENTS

INTRODUCTION

SO WHY THIS book and why two yellow butterflies? Why this book is relatively easy to answer. I have been pushed, shoved, encouraged, and eventually motivated by spirit and my best friend, Carol, to write it. It is a book to help you on your spiritual path and to give you a better understanding when you are spiritually excited to learn more and more, or when you feel lost, out of your depth with life, or questioning almost everything spiritual that you have heard or read about. It is also for when you want to learn more safely and with encouragement. The exercises at the end of most chapters will help you, so feel free to read this book in any order. You will notice there are references in some chapters to others, but it should still be easy to follow.

With all things in life there are some misunderstood practices. This book is not meant to shun other beliefs but to encourage one to live alongside others and their beliefs with an open mind and heart. The subject of spirituality is too vast to cover everything literally in one book, but this book should be a guide for you and make you laugh as you walk the pathway, as well as give you hope and a clearer understanding of many things. The excitement I mentioned many of you will empathise with on a spiritual path is exciting, and you will know what I mean when I say it. This book may touch on some spiritual aspects you find hard to believe, may not have heard of, or completely understand. The idea of writing it is to clarify for you some of the confusing thoughts and ideas about spiritual things that happen in my world. Always remember it is good if you query, doubt, and keep an open mind. Each of us needs to question what we read and are taught, and then make our own decisions.

Remember, this book is about my journey through spirituality and teachings and what I believe and have experienced. With spiritual disciplines there is no right or wrong way, only the way you feel and have a chance to develop. Differing views of spirituality are everywhere and are invaluable. It cannot be one size fits all. In essence, it is about how we live our lives and what we do with them.

I began writing this book at a time in my life when I had been teaching spiritual subjects for many years, running workshops, and giving healings and readings. Through the course of writing, I completed my Master Usui Holy Fire Reiki and a course in colour therapy, so I am still learning and gaining more spiritual knowledge; it is a lifelong journey. I also channelled through my guides the last part of a new healing modality given to me over several years and completed in 2019. Paradigm Healing© is a wonderful new healing energy using symbols, and I am starting to teach it for others to use. The world will always need energy healers, and I felt honoured to be taught it by spirit as they are pushing for it to be used.

Sadly, during the writing of this book, my mum passed over unexpectedly to spirit, so this was a challenge for me. But it was also my motivation to finish it. Mum was always encouraging me and motivating me on my spiritual pathway, and you will read more about her in the book. I give humungous thanks for her love, care, and encouragement. In the chapter "Grief", I discuss things you may be experiencing and what can happen when someone you love passes over when you have spiritual beliefs. It lets you know how I coped with it from a spiritual prospective.

We are also in the world going thought the coronavirus pandemic. I mention this at the end of the book.

Why two yellow butterflies? The abstract picture the butterflies and the coloured energetic frequencies behind them on the cover show we are to me multidimensional. There will be further explanation in the chapter "My Privilege".

CHAPTER 1

The Journey

MY SPIRITUAL JOURNEY began when I was a child. In fact, I believe my spiritual development began before I was born as I was always chatting with what I now know were people in spirit. Seeing and talking to spirits, or ghosts as some people refer to them, didn't faze me for me it was normal and every day to me. This ability also gave me an advantage; I had a wonderful time scaring one of my sisters with my ghostly tales. The downside was she needed to sleep with the light on, which was annoying for the other sister who had to share a room with her. I never truly understood why she was scared. To me it was a natural part of life, but it was nevertheless fun to create such a reaction. Apologies, readers, if you to have had these experiences with a sibling. Hopefully this book will make you feel more comfortable with things that may have worried you, still worry you, or that go bump in the night!

Although Mum accepted that I was not *quite* the normal child—whatever that is—she was still freaked out on occasions by things I knew, such as when I began making mud pie wedding cakes on the garden wall just a few months before she announced her and Dad's divorce. We hadn't been around anyone getting married, so making 'wedding cakes' was quite extraordinary. I had been curious about my parents' marriage, but I likely picked up on the energy surrounding it. My childhood was full of mixed emotions, between joy and sadness. My parents divorced in the seventies, something which was taboo at the time. It was difficult to maintain a relationship with my father, but no one was to blame for that.

When I look at my parents' divorce from a spiritual as opposed to "these things happen" perspective, I wonder whether it had an impact on my relationships. I have always had the ability to know if situations weren't right for me and received guidance from my guides on these matters. But in my younger years, I chose to go against it all. I could energetically sense things that were wrong in my parents' marriage, and as an adult, I was acutely aware of attracting energies to me that felt of a similar vibration to theirs. I suppose these energies created a type of comfort and familiarity, even though they weren't positive. Now that I have grown spiritually, I feel that we can love many people at one time in different ways, but I realize most of us seek that one special relationship. We often go through a lot of break-ups and kiss a lot of toads before we find that someone. It is all part of the journey to who we are. The more experiences we have, the more we learn, heal, recover, and are able to deal with situations.

My thoughts are that some souls have been on earth many times and may have progressed to the point where they do not need to repeat some experiences in their current lifetimes. The more lifetimes we have, the less we have to work through. But it doesn't mean we are less progressed spiritually if we have lots to work through. I believe we chose to work on different issues in different lives. So the best advice I can give is to accept, be patient, enjoy, truly care for, and love yourself in this lifetime. The only true relationship you have is the one with yourself, and honestly, it is the most fulfilling. Usually when you reach this point in life, you have full acceptance of yourself and don't need someone else to complete you, or you are able to share your life with another successfully without losing who you are. Some people seem to do this quicker and more easily than others. It is all part of the pathway of life. It does not mean someone is less of a person or more needy; it simply means that we all have different beliefs and upbringings. As spiritual souls, some of us are more sensitive than others. I spent many years judging myself for being overly sensitive. Even though I believe we choose to reincarnate to learn lessons, I still believe we must process living on earth again. For my life, I was blessed with a supportive family, including remarkable grandparents and an extraordinary mum.

As a child, my intuition was strong. I would sense when people were coming to visit. And to Mum's horror, I had a clear dislike of certain people. I realise now this stemmed from their energies. One time I told her I was going to bring home my music album on the day of the school raffle. Mum thought the draw had taken place, but it hadn't. I won, but you see, there was no doubt in my mind that I would. Another time my school had a trip to Snowden. I had started my saving and training to go. Then Mum found out that the list of children who would be going hadn't been finalised. Again my intuition was correct, and off I went. My childhood sixth sense was spot on.

When I think back to childhood coincidences, I recognise the possibility that I had likely drawn to me many of the situations that occurred. Pam Grout's book *E2* explains this perfectly. The law of attraction, which states that when we fully believe and trust in an outcome it will occur, is easy to prove when we are children. As adults we let too many other things get in the way of the naivety we have as children. This tends to block our manifesting abilities. I believe manifesting is natural if we are on the right vibrational wavelength with the universe. Although children are more naturally open than adults, they can, in my opinion, decrease or lose their intuition if they do not use it. During healer training I was taught that we develop in seven-year cycles. This does seem to be true with psychic abilities. I have spoken with many adults who remember that sense of knowing as a child and say they lost it as they aged. Children, as we know, are both naïve and vulnerable, which is why they need to be nurtured. If you have a child who seems to be very knowledgeable on esoteric matters, listen to and learn from your child. But always keep children safe, and do not push them to learn or tell you more. Because children are so sensitive, they need to be in a safe space spiritually. I will explain how to create such spaces later in the book. It may not be the right time for them to develop more, but meditation is always good for any age if taught age-appropriately.

Be wary of encouraging children to experience too much spiritually as it can frighten them. Unless you know what you are doing, it can be best to leave their spiritual developments alone. Always consider safe practices and safeguarding. Children absorb information like sponges and are fascinating if you stop and listen to them. I have a child close to me who, until about age four, clearly remembered a past life. He kept telling us that when he was an old man, he used to do such and such. That can be hard or even a little creepy for parents to understand. There has been some research on this, and a number of books and television programmes have been made about similar experiences.

Like many children, I had imaginary friends who were great. You, too, may remember as you read this that you had imaginary friends. My children also did. My son had an imaginary friend whom I could actually see clairvoyantly. He had to be allowed a space in the car, and the family had to be wary of closing him in doors. At this point in life, I just accepted what I saw. Because for me it is quite normal for children to attract invisible friends, as a family we just adapted to it. I realised, too, that this friend would likely go, and in time, my son would forget about him. My son does, as an adult, remember him, but it is unclear why my children did not follow the same path as I did.

If you are close to children and are developing spiritually, you must learn to accept that spirituality is not for everyone. And although children are very open to spirits, it may not be appropriate for them to learn with you. That said, it can be good for them to understand some minor aspects of spirituality, and it may be less scary if they know an adult has experienced the same things. I worked in a school many years ago, and a child there told me she knew I could see spirits and people's auras. That child could, too, and was naturally quite spiritually advanced. However, it would have been inappropriate for me to have encouraged that conversation.

Jennifer was my main invisible friend, and it may be no coincidence that a beautiful crystal I received as a gift as an adult to work with my inner child told me that its name was Jennifer. Jennifer, the invisible friend, was only available for me; she was always in America if anyone else pretended to chat with her. I am sure my confidence as a child was because of Jennifer. As I grew older, I chatted with her less and less. Childhood confidence and intuition have a way of deserting many of us unless they are nurtured and understood.

Yes, you did read above that a crystal told me its name. I am sure some of you have also had this experience. I did not like to discuss it very much and for many years kept it to myself. After meeting a fantastic man in a crystal shop, I explained to him that I had gone in to buy a certain crystal but had to buy one that didn't have the same aesthetic value for me. He completely agreed and shared that although he owned and had worked in the crystal shop for many years, he used to see them just as beautiful objects. He told me he had a crystal at his home that he picked up one day to give to his son. He had decided it wasn't doing anything other than collecting dust, and as he picked it up, he heard a very distinct voice tell him to put it back. He told me that to this day, he will never try to give it away again. Since his experience, he has come to believe many of the tales that people have shared with him. Before he was just politely good humoured about listening to them.

Mum had a spiritual friend with whom, not so luckily or advisedly, we used Ouija boards. This is a way of accessing spirits, but it is not suitable for everyone, including those suffering from nerves or illnesses. In fact, I would not suggest using them at all unless you are with people who are advanced in spiritual work and in full control of metaphysical energy. Some of the information we accessed was not good, and my older self realised the need for strong protection when using these ways to communicate with spirits. If you are tempted to use a Ouija board (they are sold as a game), make sure you are surrounded by energetic protection; I discuss more on that later in the book. I misguidedly played with a Ouija board in my first year at a new school. And knowing absolutely nothing about spiritual protection and the type of spirit you can attract, a glass shot in the air and broke before it fell. We had certainly upset a spirit. I can still hear the accusing voices of the children that I had broken the teacher's glass. There wasn't a chance on this earth that I would tell the teacher what we had been doing. It was an easier choice to accept the blame for being clumsy. Because of my childhood and the shock when the Ouiji board glass moved and then smashed in the air, the idea that I was somehow different was reinforced in my classmates. They hadn't seen anything like it ever, and the fact that I was teaching or encouraging some of them to communicate with spirits had scared many of them. For me at that time, it was a game with family and friends. It held no fear for me and answered questions that I had. I can remember purposely pushing the glass once to spell out something mean for my sister. I thought it was hysterical, but she and my mum were so upset that I had to admit to it. My sister still remembers it. Because of the upset caused, I never did it again. I also knew deep down to respect the board more than to manipulate it. Therefore, my higher self-wisdom—we all have this—decided it was best to keep an avid interest in spiritual matters but put it out of practice for a while, only demonstrating it at home with likeminded people. This was due to stigma from people who really didn't understand and those with strong religious beliefs. Many people attach stigma to spiritual practice. You are either thought of as a witch, and not in a nice way, or accused of practising something with an evil intent.

Sadly I attended a secondary school where, for a short time, I was bullied. There seems to be so much of it in life. When my bullying time was over, the bullies then started on their next victim. They didn't understand why I wouldn't join in. My truth has always been to treat others the way you wish to be treated. Although the nightmare of it was short-lived, at the time it felt infinite. It created such trauma in my life at the time that I no longer wanted to live. Fortunately for me, I was able to speak to my mum and a nan who was also very spiritual and kind. Nan understood me. I remember wondering why others were so unkind, but I did not feel any malice towards them, just feelings that they were misguided. There was for me a spiritual longing to go back home. Even then my spiritual self knew there is something else. For me back home is the spiritual realm; this is covered later in the book in the section about the light. This doesn't link to a belief in God or any particular religion, just an inner knowing of a beautiful higher vibration than the dense earth. It may sound bizarre, but I have never actually felt real. Years of meditation have answered my thoughts about this. A human life is hard for many, and by not feeling real, I am actually opting out of some of the more unpleasant experiences and hurt.

Some of these experiences I accept, as I needed them as parts of my learning and journey through this life. As a complementary therapist, I have seen many adults who are still trying to heal from the trauma experienced at school. It is vital that people identify and reach out for help. The lack of self-worth and self-esteem caused by these experiences can last a lifetime. Its ramifications usually stay longest with the vulnerable, sensitive souls. Identifying where the feelings began and clearing them is often like a breath of fresh air. Relationships and life experiences start to improve as your self-esteem and self-worth grow. For those of you reading this who have been bullies, I would think that your life is different now by your choice of reading this book. It is likely time, too, that you find forgiveness for yourself. My work in this field has led me to understand that the perpetrator often suffers from feelings of guilt, embarrassment, or shame. This can also prevent them having successful careers and relationships. You deserve to be released from these feelings. As a healer I cannot justify anyone having to live with pain created in childhood.

My experiences with not feeling real and many years of meditation are parts of what makes me who I am. I am able to channel and teach spiritual knowledge easily. My comfy place is always working with the spirit realm. Although there can be miscommunications with spirits and puzzles that I need to put together, I always feel my value. I also have a strong link with crystals and regularly work with them and some crystal skulls. Mine are not the ancient skulls, but they do have a spiritual guide with them and knowledge that they share. I also have an inner knowing of esoteric subjects and the schools of mystery. I suffered many illnesses as a child, including frequent bouts of tonsillitis. In holistic trains of thought, the throat centre is meant to represent our communication. When giving energy healing to someone, the throat is often blocked on an energetic level if they have suffered regular throat infections. The chakra here is described more completely in that chapter.

My childhood was full of misunderstandings and miscommunications. I often tried to fix situations or people; Mum used to tell me I wanted to fix the world. Yes I would agree, certainly my small world. As an adult, I identified this as trying to rescue people. When you have the desire to heal and help others, it is hard to acknowledge that not everyone appreciates or even wants your help. No wonder my throat was always sore! I never saw the world and things the way others seemed to; I seemed to be very matter of fact about certain things. As a child I didn't have time for people who told lies, and I would point out to people if they had. I know my matter-of-fact attitude annoyed a lot of people but recognise now it was my need to be as real as possible. As an adult I recognise that lies are often told when people are scared what others may think if they told the truth. To me, kindness is the easiest emotion to express and share. Everyone benefits from kindness, no one does from unkindness. I was always loved by my family despite these feelings of being very different from others.

You may have experienced something similar, the square peg trying so hard to fit into the round hole. I know this is our spiritual, higher selves, and I do believe we choose our lives and families for lessons we may need to grow spiritually. As an adult, my childhood experiences have enabled me to be an empathic healer, therefore feeling and understanding others' pains at times physically because of the experiences in my life. But also as an adult waiting for others to ask for help, before trying to rescue everyone.

Summary

This chapter has discussed my intuition and when I have chosen to ignore it. The experience, pain, and understanding of my parents' divorce. Unconditional love and understanding from my mum and grandparents helped me believe in myself. The stupidity of playing with Ouija board and not listening to higher guidance. The bullying at school and not understanding who I was, or my spiritual self, was why I always felt so different. I believe that the face, or particularly the eyes, show the personality within. Our childhoods shape our adulthoods, and hopefully this book will encourage you to look at your life as a learning curve. Neither good nor bad, this life is for more development. It is often why the older generation is called wise. Also seek help if you are unable to rid yourself of trauma or bad memories; you deserve a good life.

Exercise

Get a piece of paper, or better still a journal to write in. Sit quietly where you won't be disturbed, and allow yourself to focus on your breathing and heartbeat. By doing this you will quieten your mind, and it will release a lot of thoughts. When you feel ready, start to write about how your life is. Write about any challenges you have had and how you overcame them. If you haven't overcome them, then maybe this is the time to seek help from trained professionals. Acknowledge any areas where you have felt different from others. Also where you have had intuitions, note if you chose to ignore them. See if you can remember your imaginary friends if you had any. This is an exercise meant to be uplifting and to show you times when you have overcome challenges. It is also about accepting that some of the challenges may have been because you are an intuitive soul, and they have been lessons for you.

CHAPTER 2

Visions and Deciding as an Adult to Further My Journey

ALTHOUGH THROUGH MY teenage years I was still aware of my gifts, I also knew that they freaked many people out and weren't things that others readily understood or wanted to develop. Usually through teenage years if someone has an interest in esoteric subjects, it is likely to be Ouija boards or witchcraft. Having used Ouija boards as a child, I had no further desire to play with them. Neither of these subjects do I oppose, but nor do I have any interest in them. Some people may be misguided, and teenage years are the most vulnerable; it is all part of the journey of life. But like a teenager rebels, they still need support. Drugs can be an issue with so many young people; they have been something I personally have never used. My higher self knew that I already saw so much in spirit that I didn't need my third eye chakra opened any further. Drugs tend to open the third eye without proper protection or guidance, I know this from clients I have worked with and the nightmares and at times evil, weird visions they have experienced. To experience a third eye opened this way in a spiritual healing sense feels like a blown light bulb— prickly, shattered, and all over the place. A normal third eye chakra, when energetically in balance, spins brightly and evenly, and has a gentle feel to it. It is through the third eye that most of us experience the visions I am speaking about. I realise medically drug abuse is thought to create hallucinations, visions, and such, so I remind you that I do not diagnose or claim to cure. I can only write what I have experienced with clients and through their feedback. Nor have I given therapy to drug addicts as it is not part of my training. However, the clients I have seen with these issues have experimented with drugs in earlier years. Together we have discussed that it was likely the misuse of illegal drugs that brought about their past experiences. I will add here that when I have taken some prescribed medications to prevent malaria, I have experienced the most bizarre dreams and nightmares, so I can empathise to a point with these clients. Also, as a complementary therapist, I have seen several people who have experimented with some of the darker occult practices and needed their energy cleared. More of what that entails is in the chapter "Psychic Protection and the Aura".

I explain in a later chapter how my healing abilities developed through experiencing the pain from my son. This motivated me to learn more spiritually and further my personal journey. It is a strange experience when you suddenly feel hip or leg pain which is from someone else. I was just pleased to get an explanation for it and consciously know how to deal with it on an energetic level.

My intuition continued when my son had a tiny rash as a baby. I was concerned and voiced that I was worried he had something wrong with his blood. My intuition told me to seek medical advice. My neighbour at the time thought I was overreacting and had likely gone mad. Fortunately this time I listened to the voice and took him to the doctor. How lucky for us that I did. It was a blood disease treated easily if caught. If it had been left any longer, he likely wouldn't have survived.

Then when I was twenty-eight with three small children, I had a very strange vision when awake. I had gone for a lie down as I hadn't long before had my youngest and felt weary. Lying on the bed, I became aware of being out of body. I was taken visually to a very strange room with a lot of light. Afterwards, my feelings of not being real returned, which wasn't very practical with a house and three small children to care for. It is hard to describe the full sensation here, but it bothered me, so I spoke to our local vicar. The vicar explained that I had seen the light. She said it was a good thing, and many people strived to see it; it wasn't something to be scared about. She didn't, however, tell me anything about grounding my energy. This would have helped me, but I appreciate it is not possibly in the remit of a church of England vicar. It was such a surreal experience, but looking back now, there is a comfort and warmth with the memory. That experience helped me to decide to continue to learn as much as possible about spiritual and alternative things. Although this was not, I am sure, what the vicar intended me to do with my new-found knowledge. It did, however, reawaken my lust for spiritual knowledge. In fact, I can't recall ever being told what I was meant to do—if anything—with this experience that others wished to have. If you have had visions like me, they can seem scary. But allow them, and try to learn more from them.

Mum played a large part in my development as her brother meditated most of his adult life. He encouraged Mum to think outside the normal box of thoughts, and she passed this on to me. He also encouraged her to read lots of self-help and personal development books. He had reached such an enlightened stage that he genuinely apologised to someone for standing on his foot. He would say, "I am sorry for putting my foot under yours," It sounds sarcastic, but he was genuine with it. Mum encouraged kindness, as did my grandparents. If someone was in a rush and rude, my grandfather often said that maybe the person had something on his or her mind. He never judged anyone, and I was blessed to be brought up with those views. No wonder Mum's brother could apologise sincerely!

Mum also had a close friend who used to channel letters, called automatic writing, from a soldier in the war. This concerned Mum when she learnt that I, too, could channel, both by writing and by speaking in trance. Channelling is sometimes known as trance. It is when a spirit physically comes into the body of the sitter. The voice and mannerisms become similar to the person who passed. In automatic writing, the writing does not generally look like that of the person who is the host. Rather, it looks like the writing of the spirit coming through the host. The spirit should only occupy the host at the time of sitting. Afterwards, the spirit leaves the host body.

Because there are instances when the spirit coming through is in fact earthbound, not from the light, anyone practicing this needs to be well informed or trained specifically for this work. Mum always said you need to be safe as the spirit can take you over. I respected her thoughts and thoroughly researched safe practices. For a few years, I stopped this type of work as my life was not running smoothly, and you need to be of sound mind and have support for this type of work. When spirits recognise they have openings through someone, they become eager to be heard.

I have seen many cases of people going into meditation and then channelling instead. This happens when they are not in charge of their energies. For me this was natural and something I developed in circle after many years of truly trusting my guides and knowing my own energy. But still, in later years, I was grateful that I attended a workshop on how to channel properly. Despite having done this work for many years, trying another way ended up finding a better way for me. I will always seek out appropriate teachers for me. When I see the same name or work or get recommendations, these are all indicators for me to take notice. Part of my development was following my intuition and guides to help me find the right people to teach me. It is important to know your own energy as this is your personal boundary and where you need to differentiate between yourself and spirits. If done incorrectly, spirits usually try to come in through the back of the neck. It isn't because they are mean; they are often as new to this as you are. This can cause extreme pain in the neck. Years ago I was taught how to channel through a heart connection. Spirits who have channelled through for years will get used to their hosts and work easily together. Please note that this takes years of practice with people who know how to handle incoming energy. If you choose to do this with a friend, be aware that you also at times have to help spirits move out of the sitters and ensure they are fully back to themselves. You must take responsibility for your own energy at all times, particularly if you choose to do this without training or advanced spiritualists helping you. My main development was my healing courses which led to sitting in a circle, through reading books, keeping an open mind about the things I read, and attending recommended workshops.

Some ideas would sit comfortably with me, like those in Louise Hay's, *You Can Heal Your Life*. This was one of the first books Mum gave me. It was a copy of one of many given to her by her brother Roy. I treasured it, and a lot of it resonated with me. Unfortunately I lent it to a friend, and it didn't come back to me. Mum had written in it for me as well, so it could easily be identified as mine. However, I hope my friend's need for it was greater than mine. Hopefully it is doing the rounds with a lot of people and encouraging them, the same it did me. There are some suggestions in it about reasons for illness—some of which I can believe, and some I found harder to take on.

At this stage it is important to acknowledge that we do not always want to accept some situations in life as we may feel judged, or worse still, judge our own choices. The further we get along our spiritual pathways, we realise the judgement comes from within. Spiritual life shouldn't make us feel bad. But as always, my belief is that if we feel uncomfortable, we are progressing. There is a vast difference between feeling uncomfortable and feeling bad. Discomfort highlights areas in our lives that may need changing; we are often aware but reluctant to alter anything. This is often the case when someone pushes our buttons. But when growing spiritually, we begin to realise that our buttons are pushed because we may also exhibit that behaviour. So we are, in fact, mirroring. As a human race we choose to listen to many people, and although it is nicer to focus on the good and positive aspects and conversations, we can learn by listening to some of the not-so-nice things. This is not gossip; gossip is often nasty, unnecessary, and damaging to the person it is about. The intent of listening to all things is not to become embroiled by the negative but to acknowledge that at times, others are mirroring us or our behaviours. When we accept this, although it can cause discomfort, it actually frees us and stops us from repeating this behaviour. Also, if you listen and comment that the thing you have been told is not really nice to anyone, expect it to be taken as an affront at first. The person telling you may later change what he or she says. The individual may not, however, and you will see that person in a way you may not have before. These are the types of friendships that often end gently, at times in a not good way, when you are being true to yourself. It is nicer to be on a wavelength with positive people. Several of the relationships I chose in the past didn't encourage or motivate me. Most of them left me feeling stupid, lacking confidence, unloved, and at times ugly. Therefore, my lessons were learned by listening to what was constantly told to me and recognising that I was choosing to allow it. I was not unloved. I was not ugly; ugly in my belief is how people behave, not how they physically look. I was the only one who could change my feelings, and I did so by deciding to leave the energies that pulled me down. I was focused on spending more time with positive people and learning more about myself. I surround myself now with positive people, and it is true that you attract what you are on the wavelength with. This can be in the form of money, relationships, illnesses, or health. The universe was aligning to my beliefs that I was worthless until I changed my thought pattern. It was giving me more of what it understood I wanted. Think about it. When you start your day positively and happily and set the intention that you are going to have a great day, you usually will have at least one positive thing in it. Whereas if you look and focus on the gloom, that is all you will experience. Gradually, the low-grade, irritating stuff you won't now pay attention to, but even the big challenges seem easier to handle than if you start with a negative mindset. Once I started to attend development classes, life changed drastically. If through reading this you wish to develop spiritually, notice your relationships and how they change. Be accepting if they do and if friendships change. This is not always in a negative way. Some friends are needy and will keep you feeling rubbish about yourself with odd snippets of you being good if it serves their egos. They may not be in a good place themselves, and that isn't for us to judge or try to alter. This is a personal path for yourself. You may find others become interested in how you are changing and choose to start their spiritual journeys. The negative may have been part of your life for so long that realising your worth will be new to you. You may also experience times when you slip back into negative thoughts and worries. This is all natural, and in time will change. Like all new concepts, adjusting takes time. New friends or old who have positive influences will appear in your life. It truly is like opening a good book and wanting to read more and more. It is back to the universe to see that you are enjoying this new, positive way of living and then to give you more of it. Like with the negative aspects, the universe doesn't differentiate between good or bad feelings. Just that you want more of what you are focused on. It is truly transforming to begin to know yourself and have genuine people around you comment on how bubbly and lively you have become. Notice if the development classes you attend are working for you. Do you get on well with the people? Do you feel safe? Are you eager to go back? Notice the difference between nerves at learning something new and if the place and people make you feel valued.

Earlier in the book I mentioned how a sense of knowing just came to me. This has always been the case, even during the teenage years of not paying much attention. During my thirties I started to have many premonitions, some worldwide—one about a tsunami, and others about volcanic disasters. At the time, I shared some of these premonitions with others. About one particular disaster, I was told at first that I was stupid to ever suggest it, and then to keep quiet as it unfolded or people may actually think I had something to do with it as I was so accurate. Another time was at Christmas, when I said something awful was happening. These premonitions come over me in visualisations, sensations, sounds, and even smells at times. An impending sense of doom on occasions and a huge sense of fear or terror that I do not recognise as my own. After my announcement this particular Christmas, my family was worried as they thought it was something I had seen affecting us. But I explained, it wasn't us. I could just see and sense water everywhere. At these times I go into like a trance state and become quite pale. I was very sad the days after when I saw there had been a huge tsunami. I knew there was nothing I could have done to stop it, but the experience left me and my family feeling very disconcerted.

Concerned by the visions, I spoke to my mentor at that time, who taught me healing and further spiritual development. She explained that it was to prove to me there is a divine plan for all. Her father used to see certain acts in war and other world traumas. He had also detested it, particularly when the visions happened, and he felt powerless to change anything. They appear to be nothing we have control over. I still have them on occasion. But now I accept that what I see is not particularly something I am meant to change or do anything about. It is still upsetting as besides my spiritual life, I also live a human one. The part of having no control over what I saw frustrated and left me feeling disconcerted for years. Why was I shown something that could not be changed? The truth is—and my mentor was quite right—I do get shown that some things are part of a divine plan. It is still hard for me to believe as a spiritual person that some disasters are part of a divine plan. Why would they be? I cannot accept that all disasters are, but I need to meditate more and link to higher consciousness to get further answers. I accept that reading this you may feel it is nonsense or even quite a scary thought. However, if we can accept synchronicity, then maybe there is something to this. Much like when one soul leaves this world, another often enters. In most cases when I have heard of a death, it is usually followed by a birth. It seems as though nature fills a gap. Although part of me accepts that there may be some sort of plan, which goes against a lot of people's beliefs, another part is aware of other energies which disrupt the plan. This, I feel, is free will.

Brought up as a Christian, there has for me always been a higher source of vibration. As a child, this was God or Jesus. My affiliation with the church continued into adulthood, and for a while, I was a Sunday school teacher. This, too, was part of my journey, albeit to a different path of spirit. Several years later, I stopped attending the church due to personal issues and saw a different side of what Christianity in that church had become. For me there wasn't conflict with the church or my spirituality. To this day I do not follow any particular religious teaching. My belief is that Jesus was a healer, and if I have been given gifts to pass on, messages, or the ability to teach others how to heal from situations, that is what is meant to be. It may be the church holds different thoughts on this, but I was lucky. An amazing priest accepted and understood me. I was fortunate enough not to be shunned by him or his church. He is in spirit now but will know how highly I thought of him. This is another example of meeting the right people at the right time. Coincidence maybe, but for me, it is the universe aligning with what I needed.

I have since chosen not to attend church; nor do I attend the spiritual churches that are around. The last time I did attend a different church, I sensed the energy of a young soldier who wanted me to pass him to the light. When I was leaving the church, the vicar was asking everyone for tea. I was, however, ignored. I think he sensed something different in me as he physically backed away. It was so blatant that I checked my energy, and I didn't have anything negative with me. Bearing in mind that although there are sectors of some churches that practice exorcism, the church doesn't truly understand some spiritual concepts. Whatever the vicar sensed made him uneasy, I chose not to let it bother me as I had many conversations with my original priests and did not need approval from this man. This is a matter of personal choice. Attending church may be something that suits you. Some of my group who sit in my circle are churchgoers and do not have an issue with conflict. If you are in conflict over the right or wrong of spiritual work, notice what makes your heart sing. It can be difficult, but the concept of spirituality is to enhance love and kindness. To me, that is the way we should naturally live. If we are condemned for these beliefs, then I could question the intentions of others.

Summary

It should be a positive experience to develop spiritually. Visions, premonitions, and such experiences should be taken for what, I believe and was taught, they are. To let us know that some things are preplanned. They are not always negative or disasters. Some are lessons or thoughts for us to change our pathways.

The church will have various views on spiritual and alternate disciplines. Accept what they are without taking it personally or feeling judged. There are spiritual churches that readily accept people with similar views, so these may be an alternative way of worshipping if that is what you desire. You will know if you feel comfortable sharing and discussing your views with others. It takes time and patience when starting your pathway. Expect friendships and relationships to change. Don't have some false notion that they all sit crossed-legged and meditate for hours on end. That is stereotyping. Also the fact that other people often think spiritual people are weird. I think some of that came from the sixties, with free love and the hippies. Spiritual people today may light candles, burn incense, and meditate, but they also live very normal lives. Often with just more understanding for others.

Exercise

There is no specific exercise for this chapter. A suggestion is to attend groups or workshops with like-minded souls. Do research the groups first, though. There is self-regulation and trading standards in place in the United Kingdom to protect the public from fraudsters. Most groups or energy healers have some form of code of conduct. Any groups should encourage, have explanations, and motivate you. Any fees you pay should be reasonable. There is a grey area about fees, but in truth, many spiritual people invest money in good practices and insurance, so fees are justified. You will likely also find that there are more like-minded souls than you ever thought possible.

CHAPTER 3

Healing

MENTIONED SEVERAL TIMES in this book is "healing". So what is it exactly? Healing has been practiced from many years and in many cultures. It is thought to bring about harmony within the body. If our energy fields aren't strong—as described in the chapter about the aura—the spiritual or energetic belief is that we then become more susceptible to illness, fatigue, and the energies of others. The development of medical science and research took over the old main use of energy healing and advanced with medicinal cures and diagnoses for illnesses. It is good to note here that only doctors and qualified professionals are allowed to diagnose or claim to cure. The Egyptians used healing, and there are many records of how it was used. Herbs and plants have been used for centuries alleged cures. People used to visit the wise woman in the village. If we consider aspirin, a pain reliever and blood thinner, this comes from willow bark. This was also used by the ancient Egyptians back as far as 1500 BC and before. Healing was also given in churches and often referred to as faith healing. It had links to spiritual healing, but the faith came through belief in Christ. Energy healing also comes in the form of homeopathic remedies and flower essences. When I discuss it, I am referring to energy healing, a holistic method that incorporates mind, body, and spirit.

For me, healing comes in many forms. it can be from the person who spends time with someone who is lonely to the hospital with skilled surgeons who make people well again. In-between is a group of people who have abilities to energetically give healing to improve people's health. This is not curing or diagnosing, but a complementary form of energy healing. There are so many forms of healing, too many to mention here.

Sometimes people claim miracles, and they often can't be proved or disproved. Was the illness actually in the person's mind? We need to remember that clients will often have seen several people for their disease, so was it the combination of all therapies that actually improved their health rather than just one treatment model? Bearing in mind that we only know part of the brain, so there is also the possibility of a placebo effect. Scientific studies are carried out on many forms of complementary therapies, and lots of them show results that are gradually giving new evidence that some forms of healing actually work. Either way, it must surely be a positive if someone's health improves. There are new studies on a form of energy healing called Reiki; this form of healing originated in Japan. Clients have given positive feedback on their reactions to Reiki. In some hospitals in the United States, Reiki is an accepted complementary therapy. Another complementary alternative therapy is Thought Field Therapy© developed by the late Roger Callahan. I also practice this, and it too has scientific evidence showing the patterning of cells when the therapy is given. And the use of a heart rate monitor shows changes after therapy. All of these are great steps forward to proving the changes in energy and vibration that healers can sense and some can see.

An amazing book, *The Hidden Messages in Water,* by Masaro Emoto, shows how water molecules react to words. Nasty words cause the cell molecule to break down and form erratic shapes. Kind words form soft, gentle, pretty patterns. Therefore, it may be worth considering that as we are made up of high percentages of water, what could the effect be on our bodies and organs if we were bombarded by nasty situations and people? If those situations are continuous, it's worth considering whether they have an effect on a person's health.

After having my son, I used to pick up his pain when he hurt. One moment I recall was when he walked into some glass doors at a supermarket. He banged his head so hard that as I was going to pick him up to cuddle him, I suddenly couldn't see anything. A pain came so strongly into my head that my mum looked at me and said that *it* had happened again. The pain was transferred from my son to me. It cleared quickly, but there was clearly a need for me to learn how to control this. This happened on a regular basis, and although it was super that my son didn't suffer, I needed to know how to clear it from me easier. Or better still, not to take it on. This is what empathic healers experience; they may actually feel the pain for their clients. This should be temporary if at all. So if it is something you experience, then consider training with an appropriate centre to learn how to give energetic healing without affecting your energy or physical body. There are several places that run courses; the best will have codes of conduct to follow. They shouldn't charge astronomical sums of money and should have structure, insurance, and support to encourage you.

Over the years it has been a great gift and tool to be able to pinpoint the area where the pain stems from. I now mainly do this as a form of energetically scanning the client's body. This does not include touching the client. Through learning it has been possible to not keep the pain but to acknowledge it and let it go. This is all energetic practice and takes time and patience. Tune in to your intuition. If you are practising something that leaves you drained of energy, then you are not working in the right space. Any form of energetic healing should leave you uplifted, and the energy from clients or friends doesn't impact on your own. And apart from any channelled healing—source energy—nothing else should exchange between you.

As mentioned earlier in this book, Paradigm Healing© is a new type of energetic healing that I have channelled through my guides over the last couple of years. It uses symbols and a high frequency of vibrational energy to bring energetic balance to the body. Like most healing modalities, this will evolve in time. It is a unique form of individual spiritual healing. My guides spent many hours linking to me to ensure that I wrote the correct procedures and drew the correct symbols. It has been an ongoing process, and I note as I use it that it is still changing.

A healing crisis can happen for some, If you go to receive healing, you should be made aware of this. It is the point after healing when you can feel worse before you feel better. The release of emotions may cause you to cry continually for several hours or even up to a week. If you are in any doubt, you should contact the person who gave you healing. A good healer will have explained this to you and be available to at least put your mind at rest.

Because your energy changes with healing, you release things which no longer serve you. Pain could be associated with a memory that has formed as physical pain. The memory, when it is released, can take time to process. Take time for yourself. Don't expect everything to be solved immediately with healing. Although there are miracles, it is a journey. Years ago someone said we are like onions. We remove one layer to find another underneath. In fact, I would go as far to say that we are a bag of onions with a lot of layers to shift. We have taken a lifetime to receive all the baggage we have, so we will not be able to clear it with one healing session. Energy healing only does good; it never does harm. The main reason for this is that the thought behind it is unconditional love, and it is given with a positive vibration.

Summary

Because I felt pain from my son when he injured himself, I realised a need to learn about healing modalities. Healing or energy healing is not a miracle cure or a diagnosis. It is a complementary therapy which works alongside medical treatment, not in place of.

Training is given by many places. Make sure they are an accredited body or come through recommendation.

The claim to cure is allowed in other countries, where they also sell talismen promising certain benefits. The United Kingdom has strict codes for anyone working here using these claims.

Healing crises are real. Be kind to yourself after receiving healing.

Exercise

While sitting quietly, think of times that you have felt someone else's pain or known when someone hurts. This can be emotional or physical pain. Remember where the pain was for you. Did it mirror the other person's pain experience? Notice when you are around someone who is poorly. Does that individual's energy affect you? If so, you may consider training, suggested above, with a reputable trainer. If you have feelings like this, before training—if you choose to have it—release the pain from you by intention. It can be as simple as stating in your head that you accept the pain is not your own and you would like it to go, and whoever it did belong to, to receive healing.

As a basic form of distance energy healing, you may sit quietly and focus on someone, with the individual's permission, and send him or her gentle energy healing. Ground yourself. Visualise tree roots going from your feet into Mother Earth. Protect your energy with a bubble of golden light. Make an intended link to a source of pure energy. See it as a beautiful one-way channel coming from a pure source energy through you to the individual. When you begin the link to the source, you may experience heat or cool. If you are super-sensitive, you may even feel like the person is with you and be shown where the healing needs to go. Feel yourself within your own energy field and a nice strong aura. Also see it for the person you are sending the healing to. You will often notice when the healing has stopped going through. If you don't, that is fine as this is just a basic session. So if you don't, just set a time of say five to ten minutes. At the end of the session, visualise any links from you to them and them to you gently cut off. Walk around and have a sip of water. Ask the person for feedback. This is a quick technique, and you should only feel uplifted at the end. Please do not do it if you are unwell or tired.

CHAPTER 4

Spirit Guides

SPIRIT GUIDES ARE beings of energy that work with us from a level on the spirit realm. They work with us to help guide in our lives. They guide us through some of the decisions we make, although we have free will not to listen to them. They do not work like a guardian angel, who is there more for protection and I believe to help us when we pass over into the spirit world. Guides can be with us for many lifetimes and are often familiar to us. Some of my clients or workshop attendees usually ask about their guides. There are exercises given below to help you create a link with yours. I believe we all have them whether we identify and work with them or not. I would mention at this point that they are not stereotypical, such as Native American Indian chiefs, kings, queens, and the like. This is relevant, as if you are only imagining a particular type of guide, you may miss those who are working with you.

All guides are highly evolved beings of light energy in the light who have chosen to work in spirit to help us on earth. They will have attended several or all of the schools of mystery. These are schools on a different level of consciousness, where they will take esoteric lessons to develop and communicate. Any soul may have attended these schools, but for different reasons, before incarnation. We may have experienced lifetimes with certain guides, either with them as guides previously to us or previously incarnated with us on the earthly plane. They can only choose to work as guides after they have evolved enough in human form, and their souls decide not to incarnate anymore. They then reside on the spiritual planes above the earth, able to access the energy frequencies of it.

Not everyone becomes a guide after they choose not to reincarnate. They can remain in the light on different levels of energy. In my experience, a soul can still choose to come back if they wish to experience a physical form again. This reincarnation may be for things they feel they didn't learn or understand when on earth before, or things a soul wishes to do differently in a new body or country. These are not earthbound spirits.

Guides have knowledge and experience beyond our human scope, which is why they are able to help us. Some are doctors, problem-solvers, healers, and an assortment of other professions in which we may need guidance. They are loving, compassionate, knowledgeable, often funny, and kind. And if your experience with them isn't, then you need to ask them to leave. That is done by commanding them under the laws of light to leave your energy field. Guides who come from the light spiritual planes to work with us are never cruel or encourage nasty attitudes or behaviours. These are lower-energy beings. You will see how to direct the lower energies to leave in the exercise at the end of this chapter.

If you have experienced an unpleasant guide, it may be that when you sat to link, you didn't clear your energy or room with some sage first. I had the experience of sitting in a circle where the leader said her guide had to go through purgatory. Now in the Catholic belief, this is a form of punishment. It appeared that the guide, who was a nun, had passed on an incorrect message. She in fact was only learning herself. Because it had upset her so much, she felt she was bad, hence placing herself in purgatory. It didn't feel right to me, so with another lady, we asked our guides to work with her and take her to a place of further learning. As time is not the same in the spirit world, she quickly returned absolutely radiant. They had taught her that there is no punishment, or purgatory, in the spirit world. She had been still attached to her human life as a Catholic nun. This for me proved that they do first have a human life and can keep links to it. Guides have learnt lessons in the spirit world on how to work with us. They, too, have experienced many challenges, taken lessons, and learnt skills in the spirit world schools of mysteries to enable them to evolve into guiding us. They don't humiliate us or make us feel stupid. They do, however, challenge us if we are coming off our spiritual pathways or making dubious choices. By pathway, I mean the decisions and choices we make in life. Some choose a religious pathway, some choose careers and ambitions. There are lots of choices, all are valuable, and each individual makes up the whole. We can at stages in our life decide we wish to try something new—a relationship, job, move—and this is when we receive the most guidance.

You have read in this book parts of my life where I haven't listened to my guides. I often went off on a tangent and at times fell flat on my face. But they were and are always there and ready to support me when I realise my mistakes. They are not there to force me to do anything, hence the term 'guide'. They don't even say, "Told you so," as they know we have to learn our own way to live and have our own decisions to make. As we make choices, we are able learn by our mistakes, and one way to aide us with better guidance I believe is to stop, think, and then act. Also listen to the voice that guides us, but if we still want to carry on with our own ideas that is fine. If we go wrong, we will just be met with love, support, and encouragement to change our plans. Spending time meditating and doing visualisations will give you a stronger connection with your guides. It will give you the opportunity to ask who they are, where they came from, and how they help you.

My husband is an artist, and although he is a spiritual man, he doesn't give himself any credence for it. I can, however, see his guides working with him when he paints. We have had many interesting discussions about how his painting takes form. I wanted the cover of this book to be abstract. He had a different idea and started a totally different painting. Because I knew what I wanted, I asked him to relax and just allow his guide to take over. When we become too rigid we are unable to link, as described in the exercise. Together we created the cover, and afterwards he said it had just flowed for him. He is now aware that something else is working with him in his African art. It is a wonderful experience to be able to watch him work. He now feels when the brush is just taking over and going where it should. This is another form of channelling, although he is not at the time consciously linking to any other source.

I believe and have been told by Yin, described later in this chapter, that the guides also choose us. This may be because they have been with us in other physical lives. They are also there at the end of our lives to help us re-enter the spirit world. They are there for our needs as well as their expertise, so the correct communication is valuable. Guides can occasionally be shared. There are also many guides that work with groups of people for the same cause. Everyone in my belief has a guide; it is just if they choose to work with them or not. Lots of people struggle with contacting them. This is often because they confuse the signal, are too rigid in their breaths, or are expecting extreme indications that a guide is with them. They are also often looking for, as mentioned above, stereotypical characters. However, by relaxing, you will notice the subtler signals. Some people have lots of guides, but like I say, these are not all famous or Indian chiefs. Not all guides will come forward to work at the same time. If someone is working on something specific, the guide for that job will be present, like with my husband. For me it will be one guide who may work with my healing and another who channelled my Paradigm Healing© to me.

Guides are different from our families and friends who have passed into spirit. A soul who has departed this life may have knowledge gained in it but not necessarily the empathy, compassion, or additional knowledge that we may need to help us. Although some family members may take training to become spiritual guides, when we connect to spirit it is usually to the soul of the person who was on earth. So dear nan will come through as the nan you knew and will have knowledge and information about your life she had with you.

Sarah, an acquaintance of mine in a spiritual training group we attended together many times, passed unexpectedly into spirit. Within a few days of passing into the spirit world, Sarah channelled a message through one member to the group that she was happy, peaceful, and had decided to remain in the light to work from that side. She had also met with her son and husband, who had both passed sometime before her. Sarah described they were on different levels in the spirit world but got together to meet her. This was another occasion that reinforces my beliefs that we are met and there are different levels. Her message included that she had enough life experiences and her soul had evolved enough to remain in the light. Everyone was surprised how quickly the information came through and fascinated by further descriptions of the light. She was a lovely person on the earth plane, and although missed by us all, is clearly on a beautiful journey the other side. She said she had a lot of learning and training to do, and at that stage, she didn't know how long it would take or who she would work with.

Yin. Who is Yin? Well Yin is my main spiritual guide, who came through to me during an altered state of consciousness. I say that as it is not in meditation. Meditation is to calm the mind; altered states of consciousness are where we can get images, messages, and such, unless we are doing visual journeys in our meditations. This may sound confusing, but there are several thoughts on meditation. I may teach it a different way than someone else does. So Yin is, for me, a spiritual teacher, who actually is in spirit, and came to work with me in excess of fifteen years ago. At least that is when I acknowledged his work with me. Now, years later and with more awareness that guides can be with us for a lifetime and hopefully we eventually recognise and work with them, I know that Yin has been with me for many lifetimes.

As a child I had a fascination with China and the Ming dynasty when we began to learn it in history. My love of Chinese food, I now understand, is Yin's way of still enjoying what he liked. When I was in China, I had the feeling of being there before, when the country looked very different. I could sense the mountains and was oblivious to the cars and traffic. A temple we visited was familiar. In my experience, happens with all my guides. I take note when there is something that I crave or need to study. It can also be a need to travel or visit a certain place. This usually indicates a certain guide is around me or there is one new to me.

Of course we must bear in mind that, as mentioned before, even after a lifetime of working with spirit, I too am still ignorant of the glaringly obvious. So at first I was just conscious of this being of light around me when I was running circle, I linked to it and connected to Yin. At times he wears ceremonial robes which indicate something special is going to happen. He has over the years given me plenty of guidance, some about relationships, jobs, homes, people. Some of which I confess to ignoring. Being fortunate enough to learn through spiritual communication with Yin—where he lived, what he did, and how he came to work with me— has forged a great bond between us that already existed over the lifetimes. This learning has taken years of spiritual development and patience, and because I will always remain healthily sceptical about such matters, I have researched and been able to confirm the information he gave me. The information often came as words whispered to me, words I became aware of and noticed more. For example, when I was looking for books, I would be drawn to certain titles and particular words. During meditation, where I was following a pathway, I was shown words written in the sand for which I was able to look up their meanings. Dates, too, would be written and numbers; these all linked to aspects of Yin's life before he was a guide. He works with me, amongst other subjects, for my healing modalities, this book, and is a protector of my energy. He is also humorous. He also felt my grief over the passing of my mum. This is because of our close connection, and although I know Mum is fine in spirit, it is natural to grieve someone you spoke to almost every day. Yin is an amazing guide, and I hold him in high esteem. He will be mentioned throughout other chapters.

The genie guide Akbar. At this point I wish to explain that we can have many guides working with us for different aspects of our lives. Akbar worked with me for many years, but this is an example of when we need to trust our intuitions when things don't feel right. I always knew when this guide was around as he had a strong smell of beautifully perfumed oil they use in some countries. It was so highly perfumed that when he was first around, I kept sniffing the air and furniture throughout the house, especially an armchair, as I thought it was something I was using in my home. One day I sat quietly and linked spiritually to this energy. In this relaxed state, I could visualise a genie. He told me his name was Akbar; he wrote it in the sand in the visualisation. I then discovered he sat in that one chair, which was why the scent was strongest there. It felt at first that I was going nuts as it was only me who could smell it. But after this visualisation, several other spiritual people told me on different occasions that they could see genie shoes next to me, the curled-up pantomime type. This type of confirmation is good to receive, although I would say in the first instance trust your intuition. But it is always great to have validation from sources who know nothing about your visions.

Working with a genie was certainly different. Although I was unable to ask where he came from, I was able to ask why he chose to work with me. Most of his work with me was for humour and confidence in my life. However, my knowledge of working with guides at that point wasn't as advanced as in latter years to direct me to ask more-relevant questions.

In the chapter "Funny Side of Spirit", you will read about some of his antics. All I can include in this part is one day Akbar spiritually accompanied me someone I thought would teach me how to scry. The art of scrying is seeing images. They can appear in a crystal, water, or different objects. They are meant to represent some aspect of your life or things around you and to give you guidance. A little like an oracle card reading. Unfortunately the person teaching me didn't work in the space of light that I did and told me quite bluntly that my genie, who I hadn't mentioned but he was aware of, wanted to stay with and work with him. He said it half-jokingly, but that is exactly what happened. I felt at the time bereft that Akbar had gone, I was so used to him around. The person he chose to stay with didn't work in the spiritual way that I do; in fact, he worked with questionable energies. Sure enough, Akbar stayed with him, but a few years later tried to return to work with me. Smelling the familiar perfumed oil made me feel uneasy and sad. At first I wasn't sure if he had been sent to find out things about me as I experienced some strange circumstances after seeing the person for the scrying. At present I have chosen not to link to Akbar. And although he seems very sorry for choosing to work with negative energies, I don't yet trust his guidance or his spiritual presence. I asked Yin why he would have chosen to work with negative energies, and he said, "It was the lure and promise of more things and power." That is classic of negative energies wanting power! Akbar tried to join me in circle recently but moved away on request. I have taken the advice of other guides that he will be able to come back at some point in this year, 2020. He has undertaken a lot of new training and will be starting from the basics up. I haven't taken it upon myself to be unforgiving but requested that other guides arrange for Akbar to have lessons in working in a way that is good for all, harm none, and clear him of negative links. This, of course, had to be done with Akbar's agreement. I am hopeful that in the future we may be able to work together again, and it pleases me that this could be soon.

If you think you have a guide with you but are not sure, try the exercise at the end of this chapter. It will help you. Always keep an open mind, and if the energy around you doesn't feel good, don't link to it.

Earl. Well anyone reading this who has had the pleasure of meeting Earl will fully understand my affection for him and his association with me. I was first aware of Earl when I was running a circle. Earl came through me in a trance state, mentioned in an earlier chapter. He is one of a few energies that I feel safe to channel with, either through automatic writing or in a trance. Despite the fact that he was a new energy at the time, I was working in a group in a protected space, so I allowed him in to channel. Someone in the circle asked him if he was an earl or if that was his name. His reply was swift and sharp: "Does it matter?" He was so right. We get caught up in titles and hierarchy here on earth, but in the spirit world, it really makes no difference.

Earl is quite a character. He is sensed as being around when I am working with people who need encouragement and a lift in life. He is quite cheeky, and as the years have gone by, I regularly allow him to channel through me with my regular circle. I am able to do this as I have years of spiritual practice behind me and work in a very vibrationally positive protected space with some other spiritually advanced people. It is not something that I would encourage anyone new on a spiritual pathway to attempt. Remember the concerns of my mum in the earlier chapter on my visions and my decision to develop my gifts.

As time has passed, Earl has given me many insights to life in the spirit world. He has connected me to others in spirit and shown me some of the stages of passing over from this world to the next. I asked him one day how the energy transforms when we leave the physical body and how the souls reach the other side. My interest for this came when I literally saw my uncle's energy leave his body. Earl linked energetically to me and showed me only what I can describe as a line-up of energies that all appeared to walk forward into a type of light mist. Earl explained that happens when a lot of souls pass together. This is not standard as most will pass through to the light alone, except maybe with the help of spirit. He also added that they may not be aware of each other and are all met on the other side by someone familiar. There are also guides enabling them to pass through. I was made to understand that this is not the only way for souls to pass through. For me it was valuable information to receive from Earl, and different sources of spirit have shown me similar methods for our passing. It confirms to me what scientifically we cannot prove, but I have witnessed.

Earl often pops in to see some of my friends, and as I mentioned earlier, they sense when he is around. They say it is usually when they are mulling something over, but each person feels a warmth around him or her. One particular friend, Carol, senses him around, and then her dog, Bertie, starts wagging his tail to confirm it. This is something Earl chooses to do. It may change as he now has chosen to work as a guide for me, although I think this is part of what he is meant to do. Although he works with me, he never comes back and tells me anything about anyone he visits. That is not his intention; he has not been sent by me to fact find. He chooses by his own will to visit and at times will prompt me to call someone. This he does as he has been privy to how they are feeling. And although I am oblivious that he has given them a visit, I feel an urge to call. When I do call them, it is through chatting with them that they share he has been around. He is now being taught how to work as a guide for spirit as he has chosen that as his pathway. His transition from spiritual soul energy to a guide is a lengthy process and appears to depend on, amongst other things, how many human lives the soul has experienced. The more lives the quicker they learn, which I suppose makes sense, depending on the type of guide they are training to be. A soul who hasn't experienced many lives may not have acquired the knowledge that others have and, therefore, not the qualities that are called on.

Throughout the writing of this book, I noticed that when I channel Earl, he is coming through more serious. The messages he is giving are more profound, not the chitter-chatter. He has retained his sense of humour but has genuinely undergone basic learning so that he is advising others, through me, in a more meaningful way. It is fascinating to join him on his journey of learning while he still channels through me, and I love that he has chosen the guide pathway. It is also brilliant that he helps so many people. Thank you, Earl.

Sam, the adorable Sam. I was very aware of a spirit child in a property that we were living in. She was around us a lot of the time. I would sit quietly and ask if she would let me know her name and if she was ready to move into the light. Sam was an earthbound spirit, which I described in another chapter. The reply was a stiff no each time. When Sam was around, a song from the 1970s played in my ear. This was strange as Sam was from the Victorian era by the style of her dress and the information she gave me. She came from a family who worked very hard, and the money they earned went for daily living. Therefore, the modern song proved that Sam had been around for a very long time without moving into spirit. She told me the song was one of her favourites, and clearly she had hard it many times. I finally received her name, after her saying no for so long, at a psychic fair I was working at. A guy there came over and told me there was a child dancing around and hanging on me. I knew she was with me, so it was lovely for another to see her. He then said, "She said tell you her name is Samantha, but you can call her Sam." I thanked him and was surprised when he added, "I am not telling you any more." I chuckled to myself as at these places so many people want money in exchange for simple information, even amongst fellow stallholders. I wasn't even going to ask him anything else but was thrilled with that information. To me it is about helping others. This wasn't a reading I was requesting; this was about a child who was clearly earthbound and needed to move on. But in my well-worn phrase, "Love and light to the gentleman." At least I knew her name and felt her delight that she got someone else to tell me it, despite my regular asking. Part of getting someone else to tell me was also her way of knowing she could be seen by others. I was surprised he didn't comment that she was earthbound. Sam found it amusing how the man reacted, and she told me she thought he was rude.

Sitting quietly one day, Yin told me it really was time for Sam to move on. I discussed it with her and asked who she would like to come through from spirit to guide her to the light. Fear can at times stop earthbound spirits moving into the light, and for her it was because she now felt comfortable with my family. She also had communication with me, but she also feared where she would go and the process of crossing over. When I began the process of moving her into the light, Sam, to my surprise, threw a complete tantrum and stood by the front door with her arms across her chest. She *wasn't* going anywhere. She behaved very much like a physical child who doesn't want to do something, even to the point of trying to manipulate me with her tantrum. Someone who was visiting me at this time but in another part of my home looked through to where I was and asked if I knew that there was a little spirit girl standing by the front door, looking very cross. I quickly explained the reason to my guest's amusement.

Along with Yin, I decided to ask Sam's mum to come through from spirit. Hilda, a very tiny and kind lady, was so pleased and eager to come through that when Sam recognised her mother, she ran to her and was enveloped in light. I promised Sam that she could come and visit anytime but that she was better to be in the spiritual light as she could now progress. On earth she was just stuck. A very smiley Hilda and daughter continued into the light together. Sam still often comes to visit me and did thank me. She agrees her life is better now. I kept my promise to her, and she is mainly around when I run circle. She plays with Bertie the dog there. Many other people have sensed her and are aware that at times she curls up on my lap. Also, the one thing she asked for when I helped her into the light was a bow for her hair. She had seen many children with them. That was an easy gift for her. Hilda comes when I am doing rescue work and encourages others to pass into the light. She isn't a guide but is grateful that I helped her with Sam and is a great comfort to some souls departing this life.

Summary

Guides can be with you through many lifetimes. They can be from any culture, any gender, age, and era. And they are not always human. They can come to you as signs, for example, seeing the same words over and over, the fact that you are drawn to certain cultures or foods, and a sense of knowing.

The misguided genie chose to leave to work with negative energies.

When it is time to fine-tune, listen to your intuition; always trust your inner voice. If a situation doesn't feel right to you, pay attention to it. Don't try to make something right if it isn't.

Remember to laugh at yourself. If you take yourself and life too seriously, life becomes a chore. We are here to experience happy times and to live life to the fullest. We may go through periods of change and hardship, but there is help out there. Earl, like Akbar, came to me at a time when I needed laughter.

Exercise

Exercise to link to your guides. Please only do this if you are in good overall health in mind, body, and spirit. It is meant as a guide only. Use when you have the time to sit undisturbed. Read it through before you begin.

Choose a suitable room where you will be left in peace for a while. Begin by clearing the room and your energy. By this I mean burn some white sage (bought in alternative shops or available online), or visualise a beautiful violet flame going through it. This cleanses the area of any negativity and allows you to begin a safe, comfortable practice. It is nice to light a candle and sometimes play some peaceful music. Sit quietly and visualise a beautiful golden ball of light coming over the top of your head. As you relax, your breath begins listening to your heartbeat. Feel the golden light coming down and surrounding you. Keep breathing slowly and gently; don't rush or hold your breath. Keep feeling the glow of gold around you. Sense beautiful tree roots coming out through the soles of your feet and the base of your spine. Visualise the root going into the floor to hold and ground your energy to Mother Earth while you relax. If you wish to connect to a guide, this is a beautiful way to do it. When starting the exercise by grounding your energy, your body will feel balanced, and you will be able to reconnect more easily to your physical self. It stops the feeling of being spaced out as some meditation and visualisation practices can leave you feeling wobbly. Be aware of your breath and how your body feels. At this stage you may ask for a guide to come forward to you. Ask the guide to stand and breathe in the light. Sense the guide's energy. At first this may just be a subtle change you physically feel, such as a tingle on your arm. Ask the guide to stand back from you and sense how your body feels. Then ask the guide to come forward again and sense if it feels the same. If you are comfortable and feel a connection, you can ask more things silently in your head. Is the guide able to give you a name? This may come in sound or a knowing. Don't push this practice too hard to start with as you may develop a headache. It is natural, though, to feel pressure in the forehead area, especially if spiritual practice is new to you.

Whether you made a connection with a guide or not, start to refocus on your breath and heartbeat. Thank any guides you sensed came forward for you. Feel yourself making a stronger connection through your breath to your physical body, and continue the reconnection by listening to the sound of your heartbeat. After the session, feel yourself fully physically here. Drink some water, and if you still feel a little spaced out, dance around the room and clap your hands.

From here you can begin your journey into further learning about your guides. You may start to notice the same word, name, symbol, or sign. I believe these are all signs from spirit for us. Please don't be disappointed if you don't feel anything for a while; regular practice will help. Spiritual development is different for everyone. Some can do this exercise and sense a guide immediately. For others it can take a long time. Be patient and kind with yourself. There are times when one part of spiritual practice seems to elude us and then we have a breakthrough. Other types of connections we find easily. Meditation for some is easy; for others it is very hard to do.

If during this exercise you feel uncomfortable at anytime, reconnect with your breath and heartbeat. This exercise is safe to do daily if you wish.

CHAPTER 5

Testing the Spiritual Faith

HOW MANY TIMES do you find yourself saying, "Not again, no more", then you are back in the black hole of gloom, and every time you try to climb out, you feel pushed back down and the lid whacked on? Then you sense the largest, heaviest boulder placed over the top to keep the lid in place. Well that was me for what seemed a lifetime. I was going through a period of upset in my life so painful that I was giving up my spiritual pathway. Truly feeling if that was what spirits had to offer, they could take it and shove it. Certainly not a spiritual way to think. I was studying crystal therapy at the time and was placed in a crystal grid by another student. Crystals were placed around my physical body for healing or visualisation; this is best done by a qualified therapist. I was contacted by my guides while I was in the grid. I can only describe the feeling as being out of body, in a deep meditation or visualisation, a safe, pleasant space. They were so upset about what had happened in my life, but they said they had no way to change or stop it. They could only apologise and try to encourage me to stay on my pathway, which was one of helping others through healing and spiritual readings. This tested my spiritual faith. How could these guides let certain things happen to me? Truly, would I have chosen this pathway if I knew the landmines waiting along it? Being told by my guide Yin that spirit would *upgrade me,* whatever that meant, didn't do much to change my feelings at the time.

Later came the knowledge that it actually meant working on a higher, different level with spirits. The reason to work on different levels is that we develop more gifts to further help and understand others. For me it enabled me to channel a healing modality, Paradigm Healing©, which I feel comes from a beautiful source of energy. Personally I hate the words 'power' and 'ego' but do understand that spiritual people evolve at different times than others on their pathways. So my understanding of spiritual matters was to be advanced, and I was also guided to teach spiritual subjects. The upgrade was only viable for me if my main guide, Yin, would still be working with me. That apparently was unusual but was agreed on by some of the higher beings of light. My simplistic beliefs are that these beings of light are highly evolved. They may have led many lives and ruled over our universe, providing protection and guidance for spiritual workers and some world leaders. This is not the time to debate such matters as I am writing my truths, but I do believe there are these other energies which have some governance.

So it was, reluctantly at first, that Yin and I continued on the tough, spiritual pathway which led to my two years looking at my shadow self.

At that time in my life, I was going out with a man that I thought I could trust and love implicitly. This man called himself spiritual, and we met when we attended the same circle. However, when I came up against problems in my life, it was a shock to find he was lying to me on so many levels about his work, his home, his life, and even a family member he claimed died. Clearly this man was not in a right head space. And how or why he ever got involved with a spiritual group is still a mystery. I do not mean because he was a liar that he wasn't spiritual, but the two things don't quite go together. In hindsight, after three weeks of dating, Yin told me clearly that this man would go out of my life really quickly, and I wouldn't get any answers about why or where he went. This was one of those times that in my usual self-destructive way, I chose to ignore Yin's guidance. I remember telling the man at the time, and he laughed it off. "Not me," he replied.

This was exactly what happened, however, in about two years. It was longer than I was first told, although this man hadn't actually been around much during those two years. Yin was so accurate. I never did know what happened, and on the occasions I tried to find out, I was just told more and more lies. Allowing myself to believe them at first seemed far less painful than facing the truth. But I also remember thinking I was going mad. The influence people have on others can be devastating. But you see, I *recovered* from this, as painful as it was. It was part of my learning, pathway, and spiritual testing. Maybe if I had listened in the first place and walked away from the relationship myself, that lesson wouldn't have been so painful. But as mentioned in the chapter on guides, Yin didn't mock me. He was just there to pick up the painful pieces, though at the time, I was clearly still denying my guides' help and advice.

Mum was also diagnosed with cancer at this time. The prognosis was a very low survival rate. This just added to my worries but also my determination to energetically heal and clear her and my lives. I have always been blessed with fantastic friends in my adult life, and it was these friends who set up healing with me for Mum. The man who lied to me had promised her he would help get her through it, so Mum was also let down by him, and it added to her selfless concern over me. Thankfully Mum survived and recovered well with medical treatment and the healing. No one can state categorically what made the cancer go into remission; I feel it was a combination of both forms of therapy. Through Mum's surviving, my faith became stronger, and the shadow and disappointment with spirits started to lessen.

My desire to be truthful has always been important to me, which is an ironic part of my life as I have been lied to on many occasions. The desire for spiritual truth, integrity, and reality is as much the same as my desire for honest, loyal friends. After many years of meeting, laughing, loving, departing, pain, and grief, I now have a sound base of friends who have been with me and gone through the toils of my life for many years. Huge thanks to them. They know who they are.

The moments I doubted my spiritual journey so much were when I was told off for not being grounded, and when I came into contact with people who were really not nice, though they even asked after my health, as I discovered they had been purposely sending nasty energies to me. This in spiritual practice is a psychic attack, not a pleasant thing to put anyone under. I believe that energy follows thought, which then follows manifestation. So whether their intentions came to fruition through the sheer act of gathering as a group and seeing, wishing, and visualising horrible energy onto me, or whether it was purely coincidental that I was so ill, I guess no one can know. In the past, this was the problem with many spiritual disciplines. We were unable to test or prove the results. Now scientists and healers can look at energy on some computer scanning devices which show actual changes and how things like healing effect the physical body. So we are at last advancing in research. I remain healthily sceptical about lots of spiritual matters as I feel we need to keep a balance in life.

During this dreadful phase, my car was broken into and stock was stolen, I recall telling a friend that I hoped at least the thief needed it more than me. With no money to replace it as I was also going through financial ruin, I desperately tried to retain the small part of my spiritual faith I got back through Mum's survival. This same week the police came to my workplace. Imagine my panic that something bad had happened to one of my children. It was, in fact, that my car was found in the middle of a road. It had been hit badly whilst parked. I remember just saying over and over, "Oh, my car. That's okay," only to being told by the police to move it. I didn't care as the relief that my children were safe was the only thing on my mind. It was not just a small hit, however; my car was smashed into a lamp post. Plus there was damage to its front, back, and sides somehow caused by the car that hit it. A really strange amount of damage caused by one car. It was at the point of moving my car and returning to work that I broke down. The realisation came that nothing material mattered as I felt I had really had it all taken away. Even my cooker was classed as unsafe to use that same week. Something had to improve drastically to recover from all of this. But for the time being, at least my children were safe, and that was all that mattered. A dark, endless shadow had covered me.

I was functioning on very little sleep, and constant stress. Autopilot was the only way to get through each day. I previously mentioned some loyal and loving friends. They were amazing during this part of my life. Although no one can take it all away, just their kindness gave me strength. Daylight finally dawned, and the awareness came that the only thing that ever really made any sense to me was my spiritual self. All the trying to deny my psychic and mediumship abilities did nothing to help me. I realised that in fact, the further I pushed it all away, the more isolated I felt.

Because of all this turmoil, I chose to look at my shadow self. Little did I know when I embarked on this journey that it would take two years of my life. My belief is the shadow is the part of us that when it is in balance, energetically works with us, a bit like yin and yang. But when we become so low it overshadows us, our negative sides become imbalanced. We then draw even more negativity towards us. By accepting I was in this state of mind allowed me the opportunity to free myself. This is the point when I was progressing spiritually, although at that time nothing could have felt further from the truth. When we embrace our shadow, warts and all, we progress. By progress I mean we learn who we truly are and our purposes in life and what we want and what we do not want from life. But more importantly, we learn what we can give to life and to others. I have always been a deep thinker on matters of where we came from and where we go after leaving this life. I was curious as a child and asked where we go to when we die. I guess Mum didn't have the answer as she told me even the Queen would die at some point. That didn't help my seven-year-old self, which is quite likely why I continued my quest on spiritual matters to find the answers to such questions. It makes me laugh now when I think back to Mum's answer. What would any of us tell an inquisitive child if we didn't know any more than they did?

Whilst working with the negative side of my personality, the few material things I had left started to matter less. We only need so much to live, and as most of it had been taken from me, I was finding a different way of thinking and living. I suppose at that point in my life I was so deep in my shadow the only way was up, but at times the darkness of it felt like a blanket. At least the endless hole I had been in was now bizarrely comforting. My spiritual faith was being tested and pushed beyond anything I ever experienced. Working with the shadow self is something that is good to do only if you are in the right space. This includes the right network of support and love. When we do this work, we really must listen to what we are told by our higher selves in visualisation and be prepared to follow our own guidance and that of our guides and loyal friends. This can be painful as we look at aspects of ourselves that we may not like and is natural to try to avoid. During this time I went for several complementary therapies, most of which I now teach and practice. These were just parts of my healing journey, and at the time, my spiritual practice remained on hold.

I was seeking the answer to why I had gone through several traumatic relationships as I was longing for the perfect one. It is often said that we choose similar partners until we learn the lesson or get off the treadmill.

I needed to do both. I chose to meditate and changed my diet and some of the people I was surrounded by. I released the link to the ancestral line too; there are several divorces in my family line on both sides. All the relationship links needed healing and clearing for me to progress. I knew without really going into this wholeheartedly that nothing would change. That is why I stress that you need to be in the right space to do this type of clearing. It is painful and will likely make you feel low before you see any improvement. Do not always be fooled into thinking you are at your lowest point. Be honest with yourself. A good doctor and other professionals are available because this cannot always be cleared appropriately from a spiritual perspective. The upside is that you get to know yourself fully during this process. I was lucky and had family and friends who supported me during this time. They were unaware of much of the process as spiritual facts are hard to share unless the others are like-minded. It was suggested to me several times that maybe I was depressed, but that wasn't how I felt. And for me, medication wasn't the right choice; for others it may be. I was aware too that I shut myself away for much of this time. Apart from work, there were really black days, and the grief was all consuming. Spirits, however, kept my motivation up and let me acknowledge that I had made progress. After two years and feeling very different from when I started the shadow self-journey, I had a short relationship with a man who helped me find my self-esteem again and made me feel worthy. He wasn't in the right space for the relationship, and looking back, nor was I. We parted but remained amicable. Without doubt we helped each other heal some aspects of our lives.

A momentous part of my healing journey was the glimmer of light at the end of the long, dark, two-year tunnel. The realisation that life was moving and had changed in a positive direction came as a bit of a 'moment' one day when I decided to sell my house, quit my job, and travel. My bosses had been pleasant and helpful at times. But they could be really nasty at other times, and I allowed them to make me feel like rubbish. I had reached as stage where I acknowledged what were my issues, what I allowed, and what others tried to dump on me. I read *The 4 Agreements,* and author Don Miguel Ruiz made sense to me. So I decided to follow his advice and not to take anything personally. It wasn't my stuff, so why own it? Movement and energy shifts can come suddenly and swiftly, and one needs to seize the need to go with the flow at times. On a bit of a whim but following my intuition at last was why I decided to sell my home. I had been fortunate enough to keep it by the skin of my teeth, and now I was going to travel. I packed up, stored my home contents, and travelled around the United States with a friend for three months. This time had its ups and downs but was mainly a huge further healing shift for me. So many people say travel changes you; they are right. During my travels I went to many spiritual places. I visited a beautiful ashram, where I truly found peace and spent many days sitting with trees. I met many beautiful souls and had many haunting experiences. I will share more about my trip later in this book.

I returned refreshed and with a new zeal for life. Having no idea what to do when I returned home, my only plan was that I would stay with my mum and sister for a while. Mum always hugely encouraged me and backed me in all my spiritual beliefs and past whacky ideas. I sadly lost her from this world in January 2020, and although I already have contact with her in spirit, it is incredibly hard not to have her here in the physical. It is still very new, and the adjustment will take time. I knew I wanted to continue my spiritual work, but that was all I knew for sure. I chose to book a watercolour painting course. A few years previously, I told one of my daughters, tongue in cheek, that if I was ever stupid enough to go out with or get married again, he would be an artist! So it was quite coincidental—or was it the law of attraction—that whilst booking the course, I met my future husband. At that point in time, I wasn't even looking for a relationship. For the first time in my life I was quite happy on my own and had lost the need to be part of a couple. I valued my independence and self-reliance the times I pulled that oracle card. However, while I was in the gallery booking the course, chatting with the co-owner about photography, Yin told me to ask him out to take photos. I had my grandson with me, and we were going to the cinema. My hair was blown by the sea, and my face was red and shimmering (one of my daughter's expressions when younger as she didn't like the word 'perspiring'). I looked like a crazed woman from a gothic novel, nothing like a photographer that I am trained to be. After blurting out the invitation, I gave him my business card, apologised, and told him to ignore the spiritual things on it—I was still slightly embarrassed by my spirituality or excusing it as it is often misunderstood—and my grandson and I dashed off to the cinema. It was whilst watching the film that I realised what I had done. What if he had a partner, wife, and so on, and took my invitation the wrong way? Yin laughed. Guides like a joke, but they wouldn't do that to me. Yin knew what I had been through. Kevin called later that evening, and after meeting up, we got on so well that we have been inseparable since.

Summary

When it all went wrong fantastic friends supported me. I came to recognise what had to be released to be healed. When seeking closure from the ancestral line's past and negative relationships, I realised that I was holding on to too much trauma. Working on my shadow self, thankfully there came the light at the end of a very long tunnel.

Change takes time and the correct support. You can change things in your life, and recognising when things aren't working is the first step to changing them. When you decide to make changes, do it when you are ready to. There would be no point in giving up chocolate if you had just been given a box of your favourites, so be realistic. Expect to have ups and downs, which is why the support of family, friends, or professionals is so important. Only work with yourself and others who are competent in what you are trying to achieve. If you share your thoughts with others, make sure they understand what you mean. And if you need it to be confidential, then clearly say so. If advice is given—believe me there are plenty of souls ready and willing to give advice—make sure it is right for you. I love the saying, 'If in doubt, leave it out.' Remember everyone has opinions too. A dear friend of mine who is now in spirit taught me a fantastic saying: 'Opinions are like a**holes, and everyone has one!' I still hear her laughing when I think of that.

Exercise

Make a list of the things you want to change. Then create a time frame. This can be only an idea at this stage. Cross off or highlight anything that you do not feel ready to face or which seems impossible.

Add names of people who can help you; support is important. Remember these can be friends, family, or professionals.

When you have completed your list, you may only have one thing remaining that you feel ready to work on. Work out ways that you wish to alter this. It may be that you are always late. So you could think of ways that would work for you to be on time, such as putting your clock forward by five or so minutes. Small steps help people achieve the best goals and to stop feeling overwhelmed. The idea of change and releasing situations which you have accepted for a long time can be daunting. That is why you do this exercise gradually, and only when you have the right support. If you feel too overwhelmed during the changes, allow yourself to rebalance, sit, focus, and breathe. Accept if you are unable to continue. This isn't a challenge; this is a valuable exercise that should only be undertaken at the correct time.

CHAPTER 6

Running My First Spiritual Circle, Workshops, and Readings

YOU MET YIN in chapter 4. It was with Yin's guidance and reassurance that I decided to begin my own spiritual circle. For those of you who are unaware, a circle is where we connect with spirit, meditate, and send out healing in a protected space. Through a group of people sitting together, the vibrational energy is higher, which allows each person to link to spirits. It is a great place for spiritual development. The person who runs the circle takes responsibility for opening the circle and the connection to spirits. He or she is also or should be aware of energies that come through to the group and makes a safe environment. It is not a place to be silly and to make fun of spirits. It is a place to learn good spiritual practices and respect. I mention a safe environment because if someone wasn't pleasant on the earth plane when alive, he or she isn't always pleasant after death. They are earthbound spirits. They are energies that you don't need to experience, and the leader of the circle is responsible for ensuring that they are unable to enter your spiritual space. The leader will move the energies on in the way he or she usually works. As you progress, you will learn how to safely move them on. With several years of knowledge and experience, the leader/medium should also be able to answer spiritual questions that you have. Remember, though, that everyone has different spiritual gifts, and a circle leader may have gifts in some areas but not in others.

A circle leader should encourage you to try new things and teach you patience. It's a wonderful experience to connect and feel the love from a spirit or a guide, but it can take time. Everyone develops differently and has his or her own spiritual gifts. In a circle there may be the opportunity to try other ways of linking with spirits such as through crystals, meditative states, automatic writing, or psychometry. Psychometry is where a circle member is given an object to hold and tells others in the circle where it came from, who it belonged to, and other things about the owner of the piece. It works with people who have passed into spirit as well as with people still on the earth plane. Painting and drawing are all great ways to link to spirits. I have seen amazing work created by people who say they can't draw anything. The list for things to learn is endless, and all are enjoyable, or should be. Some methods you will prefer to others and find easy, while others may challenge you. Bear in mind when you are challenged that although it may be frustrating, you are actually making progress.

Sometimes some concepts just aren't for some sitters. It is then that you learn to be grateful for your gifts that you can develop and be happy for others with theirs. When people learn to connect, or channel, spirits at first may get some thoughts or visions. For some this may be in the form of a colour, voice, or a certain knowing of things. Often people will say, "I'm not sure if it is just my imagination."

Everyone should have a chance to share their experiences in a circle. Circle is not a place for one person to take over or to offload his or her personal traumas while the others all wait, patiently listening. The circle leader should take charge of this. The leader should also take charge of anyone who takes over the group; ego is not to be taken into a spiritual circle. There will be some who may be better than others, but each attendee should be valued. That is the way each of us progresses. Also, if one member is speaking untruths or making things up, the leader should gently deal with this. After all, you are all attending to learn.

The leader is also responsible for closing the circle, which includes thanking guides and spirits for working with us and ensuring that all spirits have returned to where they came from and that everyone is grounded—mentioned in the previous chapter—and fit to drive or go home. At the end of the circle, if there is time, people may like to share their private lives. Some people in circles stay and have a cup of tea after, and members become friends. This also fuses a strong bond between participants and strengthens your link to spirits.

I have sat circle lead by various spiritualists and a wonderful selection of attendees from many walks of life, therefore different vibrational energies. Although they may not all be run the same way, the concept is very similar. Some like to use crystals; some sing or play music to take the group into deeper states of awareness. The intention of the group is the same, to link to a spirit for messages and usually send or give healing; it is about spiritual development. By attending these groups, I was able to further my spiritual growth and identify practices that are natural to me. Through regular attendance, Yin told me it was time to run my own.

I was jittery on my first day, at least fourteen years ago, officially running my own circle as my nerves had gotten the better of me. Although having full trust in my guides, the fact that there were new people attending, some who had sat circle for years, made me anxious. In my head I was thinking, *What if I fail? What if I can't do this? What if a spirit doesn't come in?* So many worries. Then I decided to breathe and listen to Yin. Once I began to open the circle, the connection to the spirit world flowed easily, my anxiety dissipated, and I launched into a wonderful new space. My mentor was right: Spirits give us what we can handle.

After a few weeks working with the same people, the energy from each person gets into a pattern with the others in the group, and the energy, along with trust, builds. A closed circle is one where there are regular attendees; an open circle is one where anyone can drop in at any session. I prefer a closed circle as it gives a chance for the energy to build. Closed circles can only be created after several weeks of changes and trying different energies working together. When you reach a point where the energies are in harmony, the leader will close the circle. This means that no new people will be taken in. It helps those attending, and the vibrational energy increases without alteration. It is surprising how much group energy changes with the arrival of a new person. I have in the past attended open circles, and they do attract some very different energies. Those who are then not compatible for a closed group will leave and often find another, as it is important to have like-minded people with you. It is unlikely, though, that people will leave a closed circle unless for significant reasons.

At the beginning of my open circle, several joined and left, some because my guides decided it wasn't the place for them, some because they didn't feel they fitted in. Like I say, the energy must be compatible. It is important, too, to have some who will challenge, ask questions, never ridicule, but above all, be patient and kind with each other. Everyone is an individual and will develop at a different rate. Some will have different gifts, such as seeing spirits. Others may hear them, and some will be able to read oracle cards with very clear messages. In my experience, some find it hard for all of the above and to meet their guides, while others find it easy. The trick is not to judge yourself based on others' achievements as they, too, will experience their own struggles on their journeys. Instead, accept what gifts you have and build on them. Always remember everyone develops at different times. Sometimes you will feel like progress is slow; at others it will seem very quick. Absorb as much as you can the entire time as when we feel we are making little or no progress is often when we are making the most.

Running my first circle was the beginning of an exciting journey which led to me teaching. All those years ago I really hoped that it would be enjoyed and that I would be good enough, both for spirits to communicate and attendees to learn. Trust is the voice I hear most. To this day I still enjoy running circle. In my closed one, I have at least five people who were with me from the beginning. The other joined several years ago but previously knew the others through my workshops, so we were all familiar with each others' energies. All of us have changed, developed, learnt new things, and had some surprises. We have become a solid foundation for each other, and there is nothing greater than a group of like-minded friends who understand where you are coming from. Looking back, I realise it was healthy to remain a little sceptical. That's what I believe keeps us true to our pathways. So that first day, all those years ago, went well despite my nerves. Yin was right to push me to do it.

Over the years I have run workshops on many spiritual concepts. These have all been wonderful experiences and learning opportunities for me. I began running them with a fabulous friend Deanna. We used to have such laughs, and our energies together were so vibrant. Deanna is now in spirit, but I am able to communicate with her. Although this is wonderful, I still miss her here on the earth plane.

In one of our workshops in the early days, a lady went very deeply into meditation, so deep that when we were bringing the group out of meditation, she didn't open her eyes. This continued for some time, despite us using our techniques that usually grounded people back to their physical bodies. We looked at each other and went over to her as her daughter had started to shake her. We quickly asked her to stop. Deanna placed her hands on the lady's shoulders, while I placed mine on her feet. This is the act of grounding someone fully and quickly to bring the person's awareness back into the room. Shaking someone can make him or her feel bad as well as making the person jump. This leaves the individual out of body and feeling quite horrid, not a pleasant experience to have. It then creates a need to further connect the person to his or her physical body, so it is best avoided. Eventually she opened her eyes, looked at us, and told us quite crossly that we had stopped her from joining her husband. Her husband, we learnt from her daughter, was in spirit! Deanna and I looked at each other while her daughter burst into tears and told her, "Not in our workshop you aren't!" We felt sympathy for the lady, but the way we had looked at each other and had the same sentiment, "Not on our watch," created much mirth. That for us was a learning curve but also later a huge sense of amusement tinged with relief. The look on the other people's faces and the explanation we had to give. Many people were frightened and had to be reassured that going into meditation wouldn't pass you over to the other side. It was, as you can imagine, extremely difficult to explain. But fortunately, the other attendees heard what she had intended to do. You can imagine some of the jokes afterward about how we would have explained that to our insurance companies! I will stress here that in no way would that lady have been able to pass into spirit. She would have just gone into a much deeper state of consciousness, which wasn't appropriate for that workshop, and it would have taken longer to ground her. If an individual doesn't want to be grounded and takes himself or herself off, it will be a longer process. That is the importance of grounding as you can feel very tired and spaced out if you aren't. Having worked spiritually for so many years, I am able to work with my guides to bring people back to full awareness gently but quickly.

Later in the year we ran another workshop in a beautiful healing sanctuary. We were working with fairy and tree energies. The energy was beautiful in this place. It was only used for healing, so although many who went there were looking for help, the trees and area were regularly cleansed and uplifted. Everyone attending was calm and relaxed. We were working in one of the beautiful rooms closer to the trees. We had designed a circle for all to sit round with crystals and candles in the centre. However, one of the ladies attending, for a reason only known to her, decided to march straight across the centre of the gathering without heed of the candles or beautiful space we had created. Unfortunately, she knocked a candle over and the wax splashed up, completely covering a large section of her skirt. We were horrified, but she made us laugh as she merrily told us that "I annoyed the fairies by marching uninvited into their space, so they got their own back by covering me in wax." Phew, we weren't too sure about that, but another disaster was averted! We never did understand what made her do it!

One of the funniest times I recall with Deanna occurred just before a workshop we were running at my home. I was waiting for her and as always, was very enthusiastic with my work. I saw Deanna arrive and get out of her car, so she was fully grounded. Obviously when driving you need to be fully functional, not in la-la land as Deanna would say. I, however, had peacefully sat preparing all morning and raising the energy vibration in my lounge. These workshops were always so beautiful, and the energy was always so high. I had completely forgotten she was in a different space and not prepared. As she walked into the lounge, she staggered across the room and grabbed a chair to sit in. I asked if she was okay as she looked drunk. I thought that wasn't possible as she had just driven, plus she rarely drank. "Oh my", came the reply, "how do you live like this? The energy is so high I can't stand straight." Note to self: if running a workshop with another person, make sure you raise the vibrational energy when together! The frequency and spiritual vibration have to suit all in the group. It was also the high vibrational space I lived in most of the time with my children. My walls were painted lilac, and my sofa and carpet were similar colours, so these were quite high-frequency colours. In later stages of spiritual development, I have realised and been told by my mentors that my ex-partner couldn't live with the same energy, hence he was angry most of the time. There is a lot more involved with his energy than I will share here. When you do a lot of energy work and meditation, you look for good things, positive experiences, and this can get on other people's nerves. If they live a more-grounded life, focused on daily routines, you will likely find your energies clash. Often people on different wavelengths view the world quite differently, neither better nor worse. I was regularly told, "You need to live in the real world!" Energetic frequencies effect different people different ways. Similarly to one of the earlier paragraphs, when you are on your pathway, your friends and so on will likely change. I feel when we start to carry more light, we have increased our spiritual energies and compassions; we have raised our vibrations. Those not on a chosen spiritual path may sense something they are wary of, and it can at times make them picky or cross.

On occasions I am asked to do readings for clients. I always have what I call a healthy scepticism. I do, however, give accurate information, otherwise there is little point of doing readings. My decision with spirits and my guides is that when doing a reading, I will only receive the information that is appropriate and will never be given information that isn't suitable to pass on. For instance, when I pass on a message, my clients know that what I tell them is what I received. This way no one is left worried that there was something that wasn't shared. My agreement is that I will not be shown the death or illness of anyone on the earth plane in personal readings, apart from those who are in spirit telling me how they passed, which is confirmation for clients. The others are areas which clients really worry about and could misinterpret. I have had clients push me for the health of loved ones, but in truth, I don't get that information so am unable to share it. Regardless of how much money they offer to pay. I am aware they may be desperate, but so are many people who seek readings.

As a card reader I follow a code of conduct, and it is my intention to reassure people, not worry them. There are also legalities as well as huge ethics with these types of readings, and I believe very few people would be told by spirits anyway. A few have come to me after being given devastating messages by others, and they are either scared that they are going to die or confused about what was actually told to them. At these times, I, as well as other readers, try to comfort and explain what actually was meant. The death card in the tarot deck has lots of people frightened. I think that comes from an old movie; my sister used to be terrified of it too. However, it is nothing to do with death, as in the loss of an actual life, but the loss of something which is usually replaced by something better. You need to bear in mind that the cards either side of the main card also impact the entire reading. Because names are not my strong point, I will often ask a client and then give a distinct message. Let's face it, most elderly people wear glasses or have a walking stick, but genuine readers will be able to tell you personal things such as spirits say they saw you read letters from loved ones and even about the cabinet you keep them in. Readings to me have to be genuine, not full of fluff, embellishment, or cause concern. And they need to be useful.

There is usually a purpose for having a reading, so it is important that you go prepared with what you want answers for; if not, the reading can be drawn out and confusing. After all, there are so many subjects swirling around in people's heads that you cannot possibly expect a reader to give you a distinct message if you don't know what you want answered. If you visit a clairvoyant or psychic, you should be able to ask as many questions as you want in your time and get clarification. When clients come for readings, they are usually in a space where they need help. It is a privilege to read for people, and it should be treated with respect. I once was giving a reading to a lady whose fiancé came through. He was a young soul when he passed, and the message he gave was one of love and kindness that she had found someone new and loved again. The spirit told me about some personal things that my client was able to confirm, and he told me exactly what it was like to pass to the spirit world. My client needed this information for comfort. She was very aware of the spirit world and often sensed things, so this information didn't worry her. Her fiancé had passed in a car accident, and he took me through the moment of passing and described it as wonderful with the light and energy. He also told me about the journey in the ambulance before he passed; it was all confirmed by her. As he was such a young soul, I was confused when he described his dad meeting him. She was able to confirm that although young, his father, too, was in spirit. It really reassured her to know that they were together. He also cleared up a worry she had about how the accident happened. This reading was very accurate, and I will always be thankful for the chance to work with this couple, each on a different side of the light. He was really pleased for her that she had met someone new—that had also bothered her—and that she was getting on with her life. Through this reading I gained valuable insight into how this spirit left the body after an accident and what happened after, so I am able to reassure clients the transition to spirit is very gentle despite the cause of death.

At another place I was working, a client came to see me, and I was able to give names, dates, work information, and places where the spirit resided when on earth. Quite a few energies came forward for this client. The client, however, sat there saying, "No, no. I just can't take that." At the end he apologised and said it was fascinating, but he just couldn't take any of the reading. As he left, I remember thinking, *Oh, dear, the others coming with him will cancel and understandably so.* Instead of that, one of his relations came in for their reading and said "I have someone here who needs to apologise to you. You have just told him, about his dad, brother and others he knew, including their dates of birth and professions". He looked so sheepish that I looked at him and told him that he had been waiting for his mum to come through. "Yes," he said. Straight away I sensed his mum, and I was able to give him a very personal message. He was so pleased. Then he looked so confused and enquired why that happened. I explained that when someone seeks a reading, he or she is often there to hear from just one or two specific people in spirit. When those who are hoped for don't come through first, the client then closes his or her receptivity down a bit and finds it difficult to take in any of the message. He fully understood this and accepted that although he was obviously chuffed to later take the message from the other family members, he had originally come with the sole intention of hoping to hear from his mum. So if you are having a reading, you may be told to just take a note of part of a message if you can't take it all at the time. Often it will make sense to you later.

Confusing the energies when you have a reading with another person can also happen. When clients come together, I always check that each client is happy for the other person to hear everything. There have been times that secrets come out. This is pointed out to the sitters, and it is their decision to make. Before a session or reading to more than one person I always say if the message isn't for the person I am reading to (the sitter) but for the accompanying person, to let me know. Spirits are so pleased to communicate that they often don't take turns and certainly don't want to wait. I have given readings where the sitter has been unable to take the person and details, and at the end, the other person says, "Oh, that was Uncle—." The sitter is not very happy, believing if the other person had come forward with that information and recognition sooner, more progression would have been made. However, people often don't like to interrupt. As a reader, I have to ask the spirit to step back if the sitter can't take who he or she is, so this temporarily halts progress. So again, if you are having a reading with someone else, make all your agreements with that person beforehand and stick to them. As readers, we may receive information to pass on to you but can't work magic if the sitter can't take it and the other guest keeps quiet if the information was in fact for them until the end!

Many clients require readings because they have money or relationship worries. The idea of a reading is to give some guidance from spirits on how best to move forward. Most readings last for up to a year, so please have patience as some hurdles in life you may need to work through for longer or complete before your life improves. Within the time frame of a reading, you may have made alternative decisions about your life that are sometimes activated by the reading. The outcome of the reading, therefore, can change, or you may not recognise it. People cling to advice in readings as well. If they are told about a partner about to enter their lives, they may get stuck on just that person or situation. This is not the purpose of a reading, and I have met people who are bitterly disappointed because that is what they were told and waited for. Situations will only come to fruition in your life at the correct time; it is called divine timing. It does not mean the reader got it wrong, but unexpected factors may come into play which change your path at the time.

You can also have a more accurate reading if you are helpful and say what it is you wish to receive a message about or help with. I am not saying tell the *full* situation to your reader, but a brief outline of what you desire from the reading can be helpful. Although a reader should be able to pick up what you need, because of the nature of humans to have dozens of thoughts a minute, readings can become inaccurate or long-winded. Therefore, saying what you require enables quicker accuracy. Also, clients often ask one thing but are more focused and worried about something else. Be honest as again this will help you get a better reading.

I have had clients come for readings who have asked about one subject, but all their cards related to something totally different. When I ask them about it, they then will often say that was what they wanted to know about. Sometimes I think it may be out of embarrassment or fear of judgement that they don't ask you outright what they really want to know. You should never feel judged by a reader, and the service should be confidential; it is yours to share with others if you wish. By UK law, readings are for entertainment purposes only.

Summary

I had nerves and doubts with the first circle I ran. Only join a circle that you feel comfortable in; if it doesn't feel right, it probably isn't. There should be a nice group of mixed abilities on a similar level. If you are told that a particular circle is too advanced, don't take it personally. Some circles sit together for years. At times, groups are together for so long that they are unable to take anyone new; this is a closed circle. Taking new people, even if they are advanced, can disturb the energy and is not a personal reflection on you or your abilities. There are beginner circles. These would be attended by people new to spiritual practice. The space you meditate and link to spirits in should be protected and feel safe. It should be run by someone with experience. If not, close down your link. Your intuition will increase by attending regularly, and you should learn to develop and pay attention to it. Remember to turn off your mobile to stop distractions.

Be aware that if your vibrational energy is changing, friends and others you live with may also notice a difference. It takes a while for energies to run in sync with others.

Don't keep quiet if you are having a reading with someone else. If you can identify that the spirit coming through is meant for you, speak up. Remember to ask questions at a reading, and although you don't want to give all the information, if there is something specific, tell that to the reader. Then let the reader do the work. Confusing readings can be because your own mind is too busy and full of everything. If this happens, the reader should ask you to take a breath and centre yourself. This will balance your energy and enable a good reading. Readings shouldn't leave you feeling worried. The idea of a reading is to obtain a positive message. If things are tough in your life, a reader should pick up on this, and what you need is a message with some help from a spirit to get through this time.

Exercise

The only exercise I can suggest for this chapter is to seek out a circle near you. Ask questions about how long it has run, if it takes new people, and what they do. Remember not to judge yourself or expect too much if it is new to you. At home you can practice the meditation and links to your guide given in a previous chapter. This will strengthen your link to the spirit world. Any form of meditation practice is beneficial to mind, body, and spirit. Some circles have long meditations. These can take some time getting used to if meditation is a new concept to you. Practising will help you be comfortable with group work, and it will also give you confidence. Being aware of your breath, and your energy field is important. Practise relaxing your breath and sensing your aura. Be so familiar with your energy that you can easily identify when spirit or other energies are close.

CHAPTER 7

Psychic Protection, Aura, and the Chakras

THE BEST WAY to describe energy and the aura is to imagine a bubble of light all the way around you. This is what spiritual people refer to as the aura. *The Collins Paperback Dictionary and Thesaurus* describes it as "a distinctive air or quality of a person or thing". It is said to have at least seven layers which some people are able to see (clairvoyants) or sense (clairsentience). Some psychics can see this energy. The aura has colour to it, and when people are in vibrant health and joy, their auras have strong vivid colours linked to the rainbow that make a full, breathable bubble around the physical body. Usually we view one colour at a time, and this can reflect the person's emotion. The aura has a solid outline and looks a bit like an egg around someone. The aura moves as we move. I can see them surrounding people, animals, and plants. Fortunately for me, I have seen these beautiful colours on many people. Some are strong, vivid colours; others are pastel shades. I must point out, though, that it is an intrusion of privacy to look into a person's aura without asking first. The purpose of an aura is to protect the physical body energetically. Healers and spiritual people are aware of the aura surrounding people, and it is through this energy field that dis-ease is thought to invade the physical body. As mentioned previously, in good health, the aura will be like a solid line of an egg all around. When people are not well, the aura looks thin and depleted.

In a previous chapter I explained the negative energies that were purposely sent to make me ill. This wasn't my imagination as I had received two phone calls asking how I was. It transpired that certain people were deliberately sending nasty energies to me. These energies, along with shock in my life, made my aura very open. That is to say, it had tears and rips in it, much like looking at a balloon after it popped—it is distorted and weakened. Because of these tears and rips, my energy field and physical body were vulnerable. Therefore, it was easy for anyone to send negative energies deliberately to make me ill. Considering the spiritual work that I practice, when in good health, my spiritual protection on my aura was depleted. Not having time and feeling too ill each day made me forget how important it was to my general health to use spiritual protection. Ultimately, I was energetically wide open. My aura was in tatters, so all the rubbish thrown at me loaded onto my physical body. At the time I was in and out of hospital for various illnesses. My intuition told me that it was a combination of the deliberate psychic attack and other traumas. I contacted several trusted spiritual people, who were able to stop the psychic attack and rebuild and protect my aura until eventually I was able to take responsibility for myself again, which also enabled my health to recover.

I was also aware that certain foods had made me ill, so they had to be avoided. Food, like cleaning products, can create allergies in some people. My body is very sensitive to a lot of things which will create a toxin in me. With some of the therapies I practice now, I know there is a correlation to foods consumed at the time I experienced trauma, or illness, that created a link from the trauma to certain foods, causing further issues. This can be cleared, but it means digging down to the time they started. Plus it seems some of the foods my mum was also intolerant to. So there could be a genetic link as well.

Psychic protection is something people don't often think about or are even aware of. As you are reading this book, my guess is that you have some curiosity about or practice some spiritual matters. Please don't take this as teaching things you may already know. If you do, then skip this part. However, we all need a boost or update at times.

As explained, the aura energetically protects the physical body. When this becomes depleted through stress—a major factor—or illness, it gets weaker, and then in turn, so does the physical body. In order to strengthen it, visualising strong vibrant colours going around you will help. Sensing a cloak of beautiful blue will also protect your energy, as will sensing a golden disc placed over your tummy area. The tummy area is often a weak spot on people. When we have arguments or bad news, it is this area, known as the solar plexus chakra, which responds. This is often why people feel sick or have tummy issues. It is why some of the martial arts teaches people to hit that area. If someone takes out the solar plexus, the opponent becomes weaker and an easier target. Therefore visualising a shield over it will help you deflect issues that come up. The blue cloak allows you to project negative comments or people away from you. Projections, or thoughts from others, can make you feel inadequate or experience a low mood. You should find that using these methods helps you feel better and more confident in yourself.

Friendships often change when we embark on a spiritual pathway. Those people we thought we needed who may not have always been kind or given us confidence or were our real friends seem to be replaced by new like-minded souls. True friends, as we know, boost and encourage us. They make us feel good about ourselves. They *celebrate* our successes and encourage us through tough times. It can be daunting to leave friendships that are negative as at some point we benefitted from them. On a spiritual path, you may have more awareness of or will consciously notice the friendships that have run their course gently disappear. You will hopefully experience positive changes in your energy and thoughts. I have studied many alternative spiritual and complementary therapies and been troubled over the years that they teach about grounding but not about spiritual protection. A good analogy is when you go to a party and someone comes up to you and tells you what a bad day he or she had and how awful the person feels, and you start to sympathise with him or her. The person then goes off, feeling wonderful, leaving you sitting and feeling so bad that you think you may go home. This is a classic case of someone unconsciously taking your good energy and you allowing their negative energy to pass to you. If you use the shield or the cloak before you go into these situations, you will have a nice boundary around you. And while you can still listen to the person, you at least won't allow another to energetically take your personal happiness. These energy exchanges happen all the time everywhere, pubs, clubs, cinema, restaurants—literally everywhere. They aren't even always deliberate. We all have a bad day and dump on friends, and we are usually unaware of the effect on the other person. You wouldn't go out of your home and leave your front door wide open, so why leave your aura wide open.

Jealousy is another factor in psychic attack. Some people often want what another person has, even if it isn't what they need. To describe it best, it is the yucky feeling you get when around someone who is lamenting a lack of things and keep telling you how lucky you are. Again, like the party analogy, these conversations can leave you drained and even feeling guilty or depressed. At times people with spiritual gifts will find others saying they wish they could sense, see, whatever the gifts are. It is a case of being careful what you wish for. There are reasons why some have certain spiritual gifts and others develop them or don't have them. Now, not everyone is out to get you, but being a bit more in tune with your gut feelings will help you through a lot of emotions. Starting out by protecting your energy will leave you feeling less drained and more able to listen effectively and help others.

The chakra system, covered basically here, are energy centres in the human body. They are like spinning wheels that when in balance and good health, are felt by energy healers and seen by psychics as strong with a clear vibration and colour. There are different schools of thought to the colours, depending whether taught in the East or West. I use the basic rainbow colours starting at the base of the spine, which resonates to red when in perfect health. Orange in the lower abdomen, called the sacral. Yellow above the navel, mentioned as the area for karate and kung fu attacks; this is the solar plexus. This is the seat of the emotions and where we feel the yuk if things are going wrong. The throat area is blue, and as mentioned earlier in the book, for me has always had problems. For me, it was not until I was almost forty-two for me to balance this chakra properly. Before that, the energy always felt sticky and clogged. That was likely why I had so many throat issues. Then we have the third eye, which is the colour indigo and where most of us experience our intuitions. At the crown of the head is the crown centre; it resonates to the colour violet. This is said to be the link to our spiritual selves. There are many articles about the chakras and what they are said to do for us.

Summary

It is thought that a strong aura surrounds a healthy physical and energetic body and boundary. When in poor health, complementary beliefs are that the aura becomes less vibrant and depleted. This can be seen by some psychics and other spiritual people. When the aura is depleted, you are vulnerable to dis-ease within the body, mind, and spirit. Psychic attack at this time—whether in the form of jealousy, ill-wishing or other forms—can leave you with a weak energetic system that takes longer to recover from illness, insomnia, or depression. Visualising a cloak of protection around you and rebuilding your aura can help.

Exercise

Please note that illness or feeling low is obviously not always an indication of psychic attack. So this exercise is not meant to replace medical advice or guidance, and proper medical advice should be sought. This exercise is complementary and designed to energetically clear and sweep your aura and protect it spiritually.

Sit quietly in a safe place. Light a candle if you wish, and visualise the room clearing with a golden light. Push the light before you and all around you. Imagine stepping into a giant sieve underneath your feet. Pull the sieve all the way up around you. Your intention is to remove anything energetically attached to you in your aura that doesn't serve your higher self. When the sieve gets above your head, visualise anything collected in it going into a violet flame. Some of the debris collected may be negative thoughts. Don't dwell on what was sieved off; it is not important. Do this three times. When you have completed it, visualise a violet and gold light coming down from above your head and all around your physical body and aura. This exercise will have cleared a lot of your energy field. To strengthen your aura, breathe each colour of the rainbow in turn up and around you. Start with red, and continue with all the colours until you have breathed violet. Notice any colour that felt quite weak. It does help to use the weak colour around you, either by wearing it or if you have it in your home, maybe as cushions. Spend extra time focusing on the weak colour when doing the exercise until it feels very strong. You may notice from time to time that the colour changes. This is normal, so follow the same practice.

As the aura constantly changes, it may be one day you need more red as you are going through a phase where you need extra motivation or energy. Or you may need more of another colour. Allow your body to choose, and acknowledge any thoughts or images you get.

For protection, sense a hooded deep-blue cloak with flecks of gold coming around you. This cloak will shield you from negativity and should make you feel safe and warm. You can visualise it in the morning when you get up and in the evening before you go to bed. Visualising a golden cloak instead of the blue one around you with the hood up is also lovely just before going to sleep. Do these exercises when you are depleted of energy, feel vulnerable, or just to feel protected of others' thoughts and projections.

You can do a similar exercise to strengthen your chakras. You may even sense or see them. Always visualise beautiful, strong, vibrant colours going into them. Do not worry if they are different colours. These centres, like the aura, will change with situations you are going through.

CHAPTER 8

The Funny and at Times Annoying Side of Spirits and Ghosts

IT MAY SEEM a strange title for a chapter, but the laughs, joy, and humour of spirits never cease to amaze and inspire me, so shared here are some fantastic examples of them. I refer to the spirit as an energy, soul, that has passed from this plane of living to another, often unseen world. Ghosts are another form of spirit. Those described in this chapter are earthbound, but it is often just a term used by people to simplify the spiritual side of life and apparitions.

Not surprisingly, many of my homes have had spiritual activity in a positive way. When looking for a new home, I have often been aware of the energies in them. Some are very old energies. Some clearly have an issue with the possibility of new owners, which will make the hair on your neck or head feel like it is standing on end, while some are excited at the prospect of new people. Plus, of course, when looking for a residence, regardless of new or old, research what was previously on the land. Lots of rebuilds have happened on hospitals, pubs, and even on old churches. The land can also hold spirit energies. Some are known as replay energies, where it has been a cycle of energy. So the actual spirit isn't there, but what people can witness is sort of a stuck-in-a-loop memory of what was there previously. There are, at times, the presence of either earthbound or people who have passed over to spirit that make themselves quite well known. Part of my pathway has been healing and clearing some of these energies.

I was once on the grounds of a healing sanctuary with a friend. We were looking for an old tree stump that was allegedly able to take you back in time, so a little bit tongue-in-cheek. We went through this wood, stopping to climb on various tree stumps to meditate, to see if we were transported back in time. Well I climbed on one particular stump, stood still, and took a deep breath. Within seconds, I was very quickly pushed hard off the tree by an energy. The spirit energy was clearly cross, shouting at me to "Get orf mi tree," in a very deep, gruff voice. As I landed hard to the side, my friend was really concerned and asked if I was okay. He had seen a little fella, a bit like a gnome, charge up to me and push me. He hadn't heard anything himself but had the idea from seeing me physically shoved so hard that I wasn't welcome on that tree. We both burst out laughing as neither had experienced what the other saw or heard. But the whole situation was very funny. We decided that maybe we would leave that particular tree alone. After that episode, we asked permission to stand on any more of the stumps. It was a very interesting place to visit. The energies held there were very old amongst the wood. If you sat quietly, you could hear horses and armies passing through. These are what I relate to as replay energies.

Sitting in a pub one evening, having a meal and quiz night with some friends, we started chatting and messing around about a lady named Enid, who had passed some years previously. The lady in spirit was a bit of a joker herself, and although I didn't know her personally, one of my friends did and was describing her so well that we could all imagine her. This friend who knew Enid is herself hysterically funny. So together we all got sillier and sillier. Despite being in a pub, none of us had touched any alcohol; it was just a night of laughter. On and on we went about this lady, roaring with laughter at her antics when she was alive, that eventually we joked we would dig her up and get her to entertain us by bringing her back to life. You hopefully can now imagine, reader, just how crazy this was. We had tears of laughter streaming down our faces. At this point, crowing with laughter—even one of our more sensible friends was laughing with us—the wall light opposite our table completely shattered with a loud bang all over the place. Clearly Enid was either highly entertained or showing her disapproval. It brought an abrupt halt to the laughter. Everywhere were shocked faces and then more laughter.

On another night out with the same friends, we went to a different old pub. Chatting again about spirits, which we often do, there was so much activity in the place that I brought in a spirit bear around us for protection. Sam, mentioned in chapter 4, the little girl in spirit who likes to be around me, was playing on the floor. The look on one friend's face was brilliant as she whispered that there was a spirit child playing on the floor, but her concern was about a massive bear behind me. She thought it might hurt the child. I had completely forgotten that this lady is able to see spirits and had to explain quickly that both had come with me, much to her relief. The bear is a sprit power animal that protects and gives me strength. I had moved Sam into the light several years previously on the compromise that I would let her come back and be around me. Keeping to this promise, although spirits I believe have free will, Sam often accompanied me to places I visited and loved to play with the spirit bear. Various other psychics have often come up to me at different places to tell me I have a child playing around me. It is nice that others see and acknowledge her too.

The conversation this night, as always, got more intense about how many spirits were in this place. And it was not just the alcohol. We could see them in the restaurant, on the sofas, all over. Sam often points out spirits and lets me know what they want. She also helps take some of them to the light with my guides if they are earthbound. Earthbound spirits will often attach to pubs because of the energy there. This is not always good energy, so many types are attracted. When you discuss spirits, it also gets their attention, and they start to come towards you. Often they are pleased that they are noticed, and sometimes it is their opportunities, if they are earthbound, to go through to the light. Helping spirits pass to the light is something I have done for years and why I avoid the ghost hunt places. Such places appear to make you sign to say you won't move spirit on. This goes against all my beliefs. I am sure the people running those events wouldn't like to be trapped on the earth plane just for others to get spooky thrills! Besides which, I am quite sure there are enough energies in the light who would be willing to give a little ghostly entertainment!

During my visit to this pub, I entered an empty ladies' toilet with slight apprehension following our eerie conversation, the awareness of all the spirits around, and the creaky doors and floors. Old pubs tend to have a spooky feel to them at the best of times, without chatting about ghosts. I did find it highly amusing that a spirit decided to hold the door firmly shut when I tried to exit the toilet cubicle. I pulled the door hard several times, but it didn't open. I turned the handle again and again. In the end, I asked that if the spirit was holding the door to please let go now to let me out. Laughing to myself, I wondered how it must look to my friends as I had been gone some time, and they had no idea that there I was, seemingly locked in a toilet cubicle without a bolt across the door, asking the spirit to release me. Yanking the door once more, I suddenly was sprung backwards and found myself once more placed unceremoniously upon the toilet seat, sensing the great delight of some mischievous ghost. As I exited the cubicle, there was no one else in the vicinity!

Akbar, as mentioned earlier in this book, was in the past always around when I was meditating. His energy and character were humorous, and he brought a lot of laughter to my life. He often gave me crazy ideas of things to do. My dog, a St Bernard at the time, used to sense him around and start charging about in the house, no mean feat in a tiny house. One day I was attending a friend's workshop with Akbar in tow. When we came to the part where she wanted to take us through a visualisation, I settled comfortably into this. Relaxing my breath, I started to go deeply into another state of blissful consciousness. It was a beautiful visualisation, especially as we were being taken into the ocean to sense a beautiful golden orb and dolphins coming towards us. Relaxing further and waiting for the orb and dolphins, I was aware of a change of consciousness. Instead of being in the ocean, I was now lying on a beach with Akbar, sunbathing! He thought it very funny that once again he had taken me elsewhere. When my friend came to me in the group to ask about my experience, I replied that it was wonderful. I didn't tell her what had happened again; she was aware of my guide previously taking me off track. My mind was too active, and visualisation wasn't at the time my strongest point. This was why Akbar could so easily get me drifting into something else. It was Akbar, too, who popped into a workshop where everyone was focusing to see my aura. Sitting very still for everyone against a white background—I rarely sit still and being sensible doesn't come easily to me, so I was feeling quite smug with myself—when this voice whispered in my ear, "You don't half look a plonker sitting there!" A huge smile swept over my face as I struggled not to laugh out loud. The lady running the workshop said she saw my guide lean over to me and would love to know what he said that caused such a grin on my face.

Travel for me is always an exciting experience and often a spiritual one. At this point it is best to let you know that in my experience, unless we are trying to contact spirits, they mainly visit us when we are trying to sleep. It is the time that we are most relaxed, so we are more open to connecting with them through dreams. Whilst travelling through the United States with a friend, we shared a room in an incredibly haunted hotel. The type of hotel that makes your hair literally stand on end, gives you goosebumps, and makes weird unexplained noises. One night when we were going to sleep, I was so tired and there was so much activity in the room that I asked my friend if she could put the light up for the spirit, if earthbound, to move into. Trying hard to once again get to sleep, I was bombarded by more spirit, "Did you put the light up?" I asked. "Yes," she replied, "in the middle of the room." "No", I laughed. "No wonder we are bombarded. Please put it in the hallway!"

Trying again to sleep, I was aware of another spirit hovering over me. I asked it to go to the light but sensed it had other plans. In these situations, I do my best to see what spirits want, particularly if they are earthbound. Sometimes it is fear of where they go when they walk into the light. Others may want a loved one to come and help them into the spiritual realms. There are many reasons. This time the reason was they wanted to stay earthbound. Deciding that this was best sorted in the morning, I asked them to please let me sleep. Enquiring to my friend if she now sensed the room was clear and if it was okay to go to sleep now, her reply was, "They said yes." It was just so funny. Clearly they hadn't gone at all!

At another hotel, this time an old prison turned into a hotel, a lot of things moved around the room. We were too tired to get up and look, so we hoped to leave the energy until the morning. The spirit didn't appear to be too happy about this as my friend opened her eyes and saw a shadow hanging over my bed. Being so tired, I told them to go away; I would sort them in the morning. The reply came with the shower door being banged open so loudly we thought it had shattered! In the morning, not only was the shower door open, but several cosmetics were thrown around the bathroom.

One of the last places we stayed in the United States was a pretty, wooden, summer-type house. It had a small loft upstairs with just enough headroom to sit up. I chose it for my bedroom. There was a gallery that overlooked the bed below. During the day we visited a museum, and I bought a badger kachina doll from the shop. Settling down to sleep, there was a spirit lady who kept nudging and prodding me. Every time I closed my eyes, she poked me again. I called down to my friend to test if there was anything in particular this lady wanted as she wasn't communicating with me, apart from the poking. My friend uses kinesiology to test but is also psychic. Once the spirit knew we were serious about listening, we were able to open communication with her. She was very clear it was because she didn't think I knew what the kachina doll was for and that I would misuse it. Not to be comforted by my promise to find out about it, she wasn't going to leave me alone until I had gone on the internet right then and found out what it was for. The badger kachina is likened to the strength of the badger and is used as one of the most powerful healers in some American Indian traditions. It has knowledge of herbs and plants. As a healer myself, this confirmed why I chose this particular doll. Now reassured, the lady in spirit was happy to go and leave me in peace to sleep. Even now, this particular doll takes part in some of my healing ceremonies and is loved and revered by many. My grandson, bless him, told me he really, really likes that doll. I replied it is one of my favourites too, and he can't have it yet!

On another funny note, after several sessions of running my first circle, we were all very in tune with each other. Everyone was used to the routine as it is always best to open a circle and close it the same way each time. Mine always starts with mobiles turned off and then a meditation. One day we all sat comfortably and began to meditate. Just as everyone was going into a deeper relaxed state, an alien voice screeching, "Incoming," came loudly into the room. Everyone jumped and thought that spirit was very audible. They wondered what or who on earth it was. Some looked terrified. Then one lady announced it was, in fact, her phone! Hysterics all round and a reminder to me that spirits have such senses of humour as the phone was originally turned off. Many things like that involving electrics have happened in circle since.

I have had many other encounters with spirits. One was at a very old place in Devon. I was just walking thorough the cafeteria with one of my daughters when I was aware of needing to move to the side for someone in a hurry. As I stepped aside, a man whooshed past me. It was only when I sat down that I realised he had disappeared into a wall! Another time in a place where we had stopped for lunch, I was aware of a cavalier passing through the room and into the wall beyond as I got lunch. A few other people had witnessed this, and the people serving said it was a regular thing. This is what I refer to as replay energy; it has been there for many years. This is not an earthbound spirit and doesn't give the same energetic feel, such as goosebumps.

I believe when we are emotionally lost and truly need a helping hand we are helped by spirits. On one occasion I was very lost and sad. I sat on a bench on the grounds of a beautiful priory to watch the ducks and geese. As I sat there, I was aware of a gentleman sitting next to me. He started speaking to me, and within minutes, I had poured out my heart to him. He looked at me calmly and reassured me that everything would work out for me. I sucked in my breath, and as I released it and let it go, I turned to thank him. But he had gone. Looking around, he was nowhere to be seen. It was one of the most bizarre and beautiful experiences I have had.

At home, my husband and I often experience spirits passing though. Once he was just walking past a cupboard when the doors flew open. He greeted whoever was there and sat down, but not for long. We heard a bottle in the kitchen fly out of the container they are kept in and across the room. This particular spirit clearly wanted more attention than just a greeting. There is a story that the property we live in is occupied by the spirit of a lavender lady. We sense her around the house on occasions and always keep lavender in the garden. She is in the light but enjoys being around us. Another time we had a spiritual visitor who scared our cats so much they were frozen to the spot. Animals sense spirits far more easily than we do. In this instance, neither would venture from our bedroom. I was aware of the spirit in the hallway but not of how our cats would react. The spirit was a bit confused, which would have contributed to their fear. After connecting to it I was able to move it on, and the cats then happily ventured out. Objects often move about our home or disappear for a time to be placed somewhere else. I regularly find myself asking for them to be put back. A joke is fine, but when it stops me getting on, it can be annoying. It is all a sign that some spirit can move things and have humour with them or clearly wants attention. It is also to me a lovely feeling that we can live side by side easily with the spirit world occasionally crossing into ours and letting themselves be known physically, albeit at times annoyingly to us.

Summary

Some experiences may seem scary to people if objects move or doors open. As you recall from the first chapter, I had great delight in scaring one of my sisters. If you see these incidents as amusing and gently ask whoever is doing it to stop, they usually do. It can be an indication that someone from the spirit world has a message for you, so please try not to be alarmed. On occasions a greeting is all they require. It also takes a lot of energy for them to move things, which is why they need a source to generate from, This is often near a TV or computer. Also consider that you may actually have displaced objects. When people have high anxiety they sense things that aren't there.

The spirit world truly does have a funny side. I believe that when someone passes to the light, another plane of existence, they can still come back to visit and be around us. At times, like with the kachina doll, a spirit gets concerned that we aren't listening or acting in the right way. Also, earthbound spirits are usually more troublesome but can also be very funny. This is often because they are making themselves known so that they can be moved on to the light. After people have passed, they occasionally do not go directly to what we call the light. Some need to stay for a while on the earth plane, mainly to see how their loved ones are coping or to try to heal a rift. Often the ones I have communicated with find they are bored as they realise not everyone can see or communicate with them. Even more of them convey the wish to be reunited with a loved one who has passed before them. Spirits will always have help to move into the light. This is just another vibrational energy place after leaving the earth plane; it is just if they decide to recognise that help and move on. At times they will attach themselves or hang around someone who is able to see and connect with them. See chapter 9 for more clarification.

Is a Spirit in the Light or Earthbound, Plus What Exactly Is the Light?

THE LIGHT IS the belief of an energetic place on the other side of life that souls cross over to when they have left this life. Mediums, clairvoyants, healers, and other spiritual people can sense and, at times, see this place and communicate with spirits there. Over the years, spirits have communicated with me from a place of light and told me what happens when we leave this life and earth, my belief of going home to the light. My belief and what spirits have shared is that there are different levels of light on the other side of this physical life. There needs to be different levels so that each soul can adjust and go to the appropriate place for him or her. The light provides an opportunity for the soul to grow and develop. Some souls are more developed than others; they have experienced more lives and broader experiences in those lives. This is one of the reasons there is a need for different levels, also referred to as planes. It is not a judgement on necessarily how a person has lived his or her life.

I have witnessed a soul pass from this life and journey into the light. It looks like a ball of coloured energy with its fizzy colours swirling around and going into a type of tunnel made of light. When the soul arrives in the light, my guides told me it will be met by familiar faces and energies to give comfort and a form of security. After a period of adjustment to a new energetic frequencies and the initial greetings, the souls move to the appropriate planes for them. With the contact I have had with souls, they all describe being met by people they knew and possibly lived with in their last lives on earth. They are also met by a guide who will have been with them in many lifetimes and who will be familiar to them, even if they weren't aware of them when in physical bodies. During times I have sensed someone about to pass over, I am very aware of family members in spirit gathering in the space. They each come forward and appear to me as an actual person they would have looked like when they were on earth. They are usually quite excited, and although the room feels peaceful, there is a sense of awe. My guides tell me they appear this way so that they are familiar to the person about to enter the spirit world. It makes sense, as I am sure if the first thing you saw, if you didn't know what may happen, was a ball of energy coming at you, you may be frightened. Death to many people is frightening as there can be no expectations, only what others may share, similar to not recalling the memory of birth.

From my experiences and communications with spirits, when a person passes over to the light, they go through processes on the other side which helps their souls to grow even more. This is the plane mentioned earlier. The souls who were troubled when alive have more processes to go through, including learning how to be kind and how to ask for and feel they want forgiveness and deep healing. Although it seems a strange system and possibly unfair to some, all souls do not go to the same place, which is another reason there are different levels. I know from communications with spirits that the family may all be there on one plane to greet a newly passed-over soul, and then they will each return to the planes they came from. This is why when consulting a medium or psychic you may not hear news from all the family you hoped for. Please don't see this as good or bad; this is a spiritual journey for the souls as well. There are stages and pathways on the other side of life that all souls go through. I have been shown this by my guides and told it through many communications with the spirit world.

I have communicated with souls who are in the spirit world who choose to help those on earth when it is their time to pass over. Sam, whom I have mentioned before, has shown and told me that in the planes of life, souls can often do as they please.

I asked my guide once what happens when people who are cruel on the earth plane and show no remorse pass into the spirit world. This is different from the many kind, loving souls who pass over as the energy ball into the light. I was finding it difficult to understand the concept that some souls who have hated and committed crimes in their human lives should go to the same light as the others. During a circle when we were performing some rescue work as a group, we were conversing with a particularly bothersome energy that was earthbound. This man communicated very easily with the group, and although at first he seemed pleasant, his attitude quickly changed when he was shown the light to move into. After the group tried to convince him to move into the light, I chose as the circle leader for us to stop all further conversations with him but to ask my guide to take him. It was quite an experience for me as my guide scooped him up and put him behind a steel door. There were two doors I could see and hadn't experienced this before. The other door wasn't as strong as the one the man was put through. Yin, my guide, explained that one went straight through to a lower level of light, where the soul continues to grow steadily and easily with love and compassion. But the steel door is a holding place which still has light but a much dimmer one. This is referred to as the lowest plane of existence. People who are evil reject light around them; they often have lived a human life with a grey/black type of aura—mentioned in a previous chapter— surrounded by negative thoughts, deeds, and people. I use the word 'evil' here as most humans can understand the term. It is, however, a broad term for many atrocities to others that humans are capable of, including to animals. However, my belief is that all souls have a spark of light and can rectify their mistakes if they are genuinely sorry. This was confirmed to me by Yin when he explained the steel door. When it passes, the soul needs to want to release his or her evil deeds, intentions, and thoughts. This steel door, which through practice looked like a safe door, is where souls who show no remorse are taken. Some of these souls remain for long lengths of time, albeit the spirit world has a totally different concept of time. Here they have lessons to encourage soul development, as there is always the opportunity for them to recognise their crimes against humanity and choose a kinder pathway. This allows them in time and with help to pass through the other door to different planes of light. These usually start with the lower planes, as again they need to adjust to a slightly higher energetic vibration.

During some of my rescue work in circle, where souls are helped through to the light, I have been shown another lower plane of energy where some souls choose to go. This can be because they died with strong religious views and feel that in life they didn't fulfil what was expected, or broke certain religious beliefs. They may have chosen to punish themselves as they don't feel they are worthy to go into the light, or in religious concepts, into heaven. Self-limiting beliefs, in my opinion, hold them there. I once rescued a young girl who took her own life. Her religious beliefs were so judgmental on suicide that she chose to put herself on a lower plane in the spirit world. Even though she would have been guided at the time, it is a choice by the soul. My rescue work for this was to connect to her energy and trace where in the spiritual world her soul was. This is another form of meditation, visualisation, communication, and rescue not involving an earthbound energy. When I discussed with her that she was forgiven, as she was aware that one of her close friends felt the guilt and pain of not being able to help her when she was alive, she came with me in the meditation and let me cross her over to a higher plane of light. This young lady then came back with a very clear, distinct message that her friend accepted and understood. The spirit now looked radiant as she had found the strength to forgive herself and accept forgiveness from those left behind. Her friend on the earth plane finally felt at peace with her passing.

So how do we tell the difference between an earthbound spirit, or what can be perceived as a ghost, and a soul that has crossed over? Usually it is straightforward. An energy that comes from the light will have knowledge of you that you may not have shared with anyone else. The energy is usually gentle and loving. However, if a soul remains on the earth plane, as in being earthbound, the energy feels very different. Like with Sam, who knew all the modern things but was dressed in Victorian clothing. She wasn't able to go far from the house we lived in. I think part of it was fear of the outside; life had changed hugely from when she was alive. Through communication with her, she told me about her father's work and her mother, Hilda. She enjoyed living in my home because I could communicate with her, and she loved being around my children. Sam had died very young, but because she wanted her mother so much and was confused at the time of her death, she remained earthbound. Hilda, however, had moved into the light after her death and had expected to meet up with Sam. This was why Yin told me it was time for Sam to pass into the light as Hilda was able to come for her and help her through. As you read before, Sam was stubborn when it came to move her on. This was anxiety as to what would happen. Sam had been earthbound for so long that she feared what would happen next. Reassurance needs to be made to spirits to lessen their fears. Plus, as in Sam's case, an agreement that I am happy for her to work with and be around me when she likes.

The energy of someone earthbound feels denser. Again they can be loving and kind if they were like that in life, or they can be mean and nasty—again if that was their personalities in life. Most of the souls will attend their own funerals and be able to communicate the details of it through a medium, a person who can communicate with spirits. They will not have any knowledge of the other side, though, and will only have the knowledge of everyday things here on earth. Any advice they give will be their own or what they have listened to. They may have chosen to stay on the earth plane through fear of where they would go, leaving behind loved ones, confusion after a sudden death, or just to hang around. The light that was strong around their passing may have closed, though this is rare. Families and friends may be so desperate not to lose them that they hold them unintentionally here. This mainly happens, I understand, with famous people who attract a lot of attention and mass hysteria when they die. This is not a lasting state for any souls as they will be given many opportunities to pass into the levels of light.

Another way I am aware of the distinction between the two is that an earthbound spirit will let me feel pain as a reflection of his or her own. For example, if someone had an issue with their right hip, I will feel discomfort in my left hip. For a soul that is in the light, I am made aware of where the pain would have been on the side it was, but I don't feel the same pain. This isn't meant to suggest that souls are still in pain as spirits have advised me the pain has gone. It is to be able to communicate in certain ways, one of which is to be identified by loved ones left behind. Old furniture, shops, theatres, battlefields, churches, and many other places have a lot of earthbound energies in them. They also have a lot of spiritual people doing rescue work to help them move on. Again, it feels a hard or even worrying concept that people could be stuck energies, but they will always be shown the light and find a way or guardian to eventually take them to it. Some earthbound spirits enjoy just being around, and like I have mentioned before, some may then get bored. These are the earthbound who come to someone's attention and receive help to pass over.

Summary

The light has different levels, also referred to as planes. Some souls move instantly to the light; others for a variety of reasons need rescue work. This is done by spiritual people with a knowledge of it.

Some of the nastier energies will be taken to a holding place. All souls will learn and grow spiritually. Some will choose to reincarnate, and some will choose to stay in spirit.

Earthbound spirits happen because they missed the opportunity to go to the light when it first opened or have chosen for various reasons to stay around. All will at some point get the opportunity to move into it.

There will always be differing opinions and views as to what happens after death. Allow your own thoughts. Mine are based on knowledge, experience, and research through meditation and altered states of consciousness.

Do not assume that because you grieved so hard for a loved one that he or she has become earthbound. There is a lot more to that concept than I am able to share here.

Exercise

It is difficult and unwise of me to give you an exercise for this chapter. You may, however, notice different feelings in various places. Pay attention to them, and listen to your intuition. If you sense a departed loved one is trying to contact you, don't automatically think he or she is earthbound.

CHAPTER 10

The Heightened Senses of Animals

ANIMALS ARE INCREDIBLY susceptible to spirit and other energies. If you have been around a cat, you may have noticed that there are some people they are drawn to and others they will ignore or hiss at. Usually the old wives' tale is that a cat will sit on the person who doesn't like them. It has been the case in my home on many occasions. Although I will add the people are very nice, but they often admit to not liking cats. I guess it is everyone's choice, but being a complete animal lover, I can't quite bring myself to understand it. Particularly with my Abraham. He is a black-and-white moggie with the most beautiful face and nature ever. Mitsi, his sister, is fluffier than Abraham but nowhere near as affectionate with strangers. Abraham doesn't follow the thought of sitting on people he doesn't like; he usually sits on people who are in need of some form of healing. Due to some of the work I do, Abraham lets me know if some of the energies around are not pleasant. His reaction to some clients lets me know what negative energies are around the client before I even start work on the person. After I have worked with the individual, which usually includes clearing the vibrational energy, Abraham comes back into the room, providing the client is fine with cats, and makes a fuss around him or her. I will add, negative energy isn't evil. It can be the client lives with people who constantly argue or aren't very nice characters. The client may also be overrun with anxiety or fear.

At night Abraham chooses various positions to sleep next to me. His favoured position is usually across the top of my head. I think spiritually he is protecting my crown chakra, although I am aware lots of cats do this. Kevin, my husband, and I laugh as we bought an extra-large bed just to allow space for Abraham and Mitsi to sleep on! When my mum passed, it was such a difficult time. I woke one morning to both cats asleep on either side of my head, like ear muffs. They definitely sensed how sad I was and tried to comfort me.

One time I was visiting a friend for a meal having never been to her home before. I was delighted to see she had a beautiful cat which came up to me and decided to sit on my lap. I love cats, so I was really pleased and made a fuss. I then became aware that it wanted some healing. I mentioned it to my friend, who is also a healer. "Oh, yes", she replied. "Please do." So there I was with this little fur bundle on my lap, lapping up the healing energy. When the flow of energy stopped, off jumped the cat. Fair enough. But then when I went to stroke it, the cat poked his nose in the air and turned his back on me. My friend roared with laughter. "Oh," she told me, "that is what he always does!" It was so funny. She found it highly amusing that the cat even got on my lap in the first place; he apparently didn't like anyone! It had also never before climbed on to anyone's lap, so in a way, I was privileged.

Animals can sense when we have healing abilities, regardless of whether we are trained in them or not. I have worked with several dogs in need of healing. I always request that the vet be asked and advised first as there are strict laws on veterinary practice in the United Kingdom. One dog I worked with showed me where his tumour was. He was usually a bonker's dog but used to lie down and totally relax for healing. The vet was amazed that the tumour shrunk a little and said it was great to have complementary treatment alongside the conventional medicine. The dog hadn't at that time started his chemotherapy but was on medication. This same dog told me when he would pass; it was to be a year or so after the tumour. As I was great friends with the owner at that time, I was called when he was passing. When I arrived, I could see his energy standing next to his physical body, wagging his tail. My friend was so distressed. I told her he really was fine as his tail was wagging. She, too, believed in something other than death and was very spiritual herself. He died within minutes of telling her. He then told me energetically to tell her about two balls, one green and one orange. He kept nudging the green one away. When I told her, she laughed and said, "He really is telling you. He had those balls as a puppy. He hated the green one and would only play with the orange one!" It comforted her to know that he was okay and wagging his tail. But like with any pet or human, our relationships with them are so close that we grieve them. In several readings over the years, pets have come forward in the reading. The owners are delighted and love that the animals also have a place in the spirit world.

During my healer training, there was a close friend of mine, Deanna, mentioned earlier in the book, on the same course. She was trained in Reiki but was now learning spiritual healing, so she knew something about energy and the transference. Transference is when the pain or energy from another person, soul, or animal will literally transfer into another person. Deanna was also incredibly funny and kind. There was also a different group of healer workshops that Deanna attended. In that group there was one lady Deanna suspected based on her comments and actions, who was living on ego. The lady merrily told the group that she was going to give healing to a horse. Of course that was to be complementary, and I don't know the full saga of how, but I do know that Deanna had hysterics because this lady showed off so much about *curing* the horse that she was not in the right space at all. Her mind was set on telling everyone how amazing she was. Within days of so-called healing the horse, the woman went down with such depleted energy and was hoarse. It was reported that the actual horse was now very healthy and clearly much better, but the healer had to go to bed for several days. Spirits *do* have senses of humour, as I have said before, and they also keep our egos in check. This lady learnt her lesson and became more grounded in her actions. Plus, she began to listen to what she was taught. Deanna hadn't laughed because the woman became ill but because she wouldn't listen to anyone until this happened to her.

Bertie is my best friend's Carol's dog. He is a small dog with huge spiritual awareness. When we sit circle, Bertie has his bed underneath the table. He will at times come up to me and let me know different energies that come in the group. If we have earthbound energies, he comes up and puts his paw on my lap. I thank him, and he returns to his bed. It is quite amazing to see. I can sense these energies, and it is fantastic that he can sense them too. He likes to make sure I have noticed them and plays his part as such. *Never* underestimate the powers of the pooch.

One time after circle at Bertie's home, a nasty energy came around me when the door was opened. Bertie stood, barked, and actually *growled* at me. This was something that he had never done. Carol and I realised we needed to clear off the energy as it was quite clearly upsetting Bertie.

We saged, cleared, and then my guides took it to the holding place. It took quite a while to do this as there were several energies. Each time between clearings, Bertie barked and growled until eventually he wagged his tail, sat, and waited for his treat. He really is a very sensitive dog.

When I do remote viewing work—that is, working without being at the place or with the person—I have in the past been aware of Bertie's energy coming to work with me. Carol is happy with this and knows it is Bertie's choice. On one occasion we had completed some rescue work, and I was aware that Bertie had gone to sit by his treat pot. I texted my friend to say Bertie had just helped me and wanted a treat as a thank you. Back came a swift reply that she wondered why he had gone to where his treats were kept and sat down expectantly. So you see, animals definitely sense things and can work with us remotely as well.

Years ago, when I was holidaying with my children in the United States, frogs were singing their hearts out on a lake near us. We had arrived just before Hurricane Katrina did. Those frogs stopped their singing a short time before the hurricane hit. It was most bizarre, and I knew then that they were far more linked to the universe than humans are.

Summary

There are times when animals play their roles and are aware of spirits. They will often sense spirits before we do as they are very sensitive to energy. This is why they react to storms and other forms of weather before they arrive. Animals have a much stronger sixth sense than we do.

Exercise

If you have a pet, begin to journal when he or she responds and how your pet responds to different energies. Notice how your pet reacts to people in your home. See if they change how he or she is to others. If you have a dog, and take him or her out for walks and notice if there are certain places or people your dog tries to avoid. Watch how cats often sit and stare at something you may not be able to see. Make a note of it. The more you journal, the more you will understand what is going on around your pet.

CHAPTER 11

My Privilege and the Yellow Butterflies

THROUGHOUT MY LIFE I have been blessed with meeting and befriending many people from many countries and with many different beliefs. My life, beliefs, and reasoning are that we are all one of the same whole, just different shapes, sizes, and genders. Or we may speak different languages. Spirits do not differentiate between us. To them it doesn't matter what job we do or where we live. But it does matter how we live. Spirits will always encourage us to be kind, loving, and compassionate. They will always want the best for us. When my father left the family when I was a child, we were blessed with aunts, uncles, and grandparents who helped Mum and encouraged us as a family to do well.

You will have read about my spirit guides in chapter 4. I have been so privileged on the whole to have had so many gifted mentors, and that includes mentors on the earth plane who have helped me with my spiritual development. True mentors encourage you to learn, study, do your best, and to leave your ego at the door but keep your passion. They will coax you into trying new avenues and encourage you to accept if something isn't right for you. They will be generous, motivating, and there to listen to you if things are muddled. Confusion is often the case with spiritual development. When you follow this pathway, it is exciting. The wish to learn new things is so great and the subject so vast that a true mentor will keep you encouraged whilst also keeping you grounded. They won't have jealousy and will actively encourage you to be good at something that may be natural for you but difficult for them. True mentors will also acknowledge when they have taken you as far as they can and encourage you to find a new mentor to further your development. It is good to ask questions and query things as all of us are learning. If we are never questioned or question others, then we may become complacent, and our own learning will lack development. I truly believe there will always be more to learn and to share. Similarly to the person running the circle, you need to get on with your mentor or tutor; a personality or energy clash would hinder development. You may think it strange that clashes can happen, but realistically, we are all made of energy and the effect of one person's energy on another is unique. Our energy fields are as unique as our fingerprints. Because our energies are personal to us and different for each person, clashes can occur. Just because people are spiritual doesn't mean they will all get on. I covered more about our reactions to others in chapter 7. We are, don't forget, human, and with this comes our personalities. Each of us is unique, and while one person may decide on a clairvoyant pathway, another may have none of those skills required but have an interest in angels. The spiritual world we work in is as diverse as the natural world. There is no right or wrong, only what is individually appropriate for us.

During my spiritual growth—and yes, it is still growing—each of my mentors had something different to share with me. Each circle I attended was different with each leader; there is no right or wrong, just a difference. Everyone who takes part also teaches and learns from the others. I sat circle with one group for several years and then moved to another. They were quite different, and it was wonderful to participate with various practices and people. One I passed from in relatively quickly. It wasn't that the people were bad, it was just that the energy wasn't right for me. You will learn to intuit your feelings and gain confidence to change and seek out new ventures, people, and places. Courses, workshops, and retreats all help with moving forward and give great opportunities to learn new skills. There are many good teachers out there. Most come to you by intuition, reading something that you hadn't noticed before, the signs we receive. Privilege doesn't come through how much money we have acquired. I believe it comes through knowledge and what we do with it.

Over the years I have been privileged to read and connect with spirits for many clients. There have been so many that I give thanks to them all.

To be able to communicate with the other side is to me a blessed position and one I hold with great respect. One communication in particular I will always recall was when I channelled a letter from a young man in spirit for his mum. I will refer to him as Stan to protect his privacy. I knew nothing about him. I just sat and started writing. The urgency of his message flowed very quickly. He described how he felt and that he needed to say he was sorry. Luckily he let me know who the letter was for as I was completely unaware of the lady and this young man, I trusted what I was given. Very tentatively I asked a relation of his mum's if the name made any sense to them. Yes. The person would tell his mum and give her the letter. She was so pleased with the letter; it made full sense. I was able to sit with her and give her more information about him. Usually when a spirit is working with me, I am sitting with a relative. In this instance, Stan just popped in. This was an amazing opportunity for her and a unique healing journey. Through Stan's letter she was able to understand why he had chosen his pathway and what had truly happened to him. These types of communication for me are so special. They allow people to have some form of closure and belief in better things.

At the beginning and throughout this book I referred to an aunt and uncle of mine who helped us during our childhoods, like second parents. My aunt had died some years previously, but it is one of my greatest but sad privileges to have been with my uncle when he passed into the spirit world. He was a very kind man and so funny. We had such a wonderful childhood with his antics. He and my aunt had been together since they were five years old. As she died a few years before, he missed her daily. My sister and I regularly spoke to him and on one occasion, we went to visit him. He had previously travelled to us as he lived further away. We promised we would go to lunch with him again when the weather was better.

In the meantime, he had damaged his car. He told us he went down a pothole. However, when the full story unfurled, we then found out that the pothole was a ditch. And the kind person he said had given him a lift home was in fact an ambulance crew! Imagine our surprise when we found out. He really was fiercely independent and knew we would have gone up sooner to see him. Looking back, I realise how cagey he was when mentioning the car repair. I had mentioned several times that it was a long time for a wheel repair.

Taking his reassurance that he was fine, we left it that we would visit later in the year. However, the spirit world had other ideas. Although we knew he had cancer, we didn't expect it to advance so quickly, and my sister sadly received a call to say he was dying. He was a very proud man and had been with us and guided us like a father all our lives. Now all we hoped for was that he would allow us to sit with him while he passed from this world. We were lucky that we arrived quickly as they were making the decision to put him into a hospice. The transition to it went easily, and the staff was so amazing. They really helped. Uncle passed very quickly to the last stages of life while we were with him. I still wonder if he did that to spare us. While sitting quietly with him, I was aware of the energy of an earthbound gentleman in spirit enter the room. It was quite funny to watch as my uncle lifted his hand to shoo him out. With that gesture I knew my uncle was also sensing a spirit. I told him it was fine and put up the light for the gentleman to pass into. In my experience, when a soul is ready to depart this world for the next, there is a gathering of spirits to take the soul. The person passing over becomes more sensitive to the energies as he or she leaves the physical body. Most of these are familiar. They may have been a partner or parent. Some have had friends, and I have also witnessed animals around. This reassures the soul that it is safe to go, and the individual is accompanied to the spirit world. Understandably there are people who are fearful of dying and what happens, so when they experience the gathering energies, they calm down and are reassured. For me it is a natural experience as I have been privileged to see and be told the experience for myself.

This doesn't replace the feelings of grief and sadness when someone departs. When I lost my mum during the writing of this book, although acutely aware of the process of death, the grief at times was and still will be unbearable. Understandably we want our loved ones in this dimension with us. I was very aware of spirit from my uncle's family gathering in the light, getting ready to welcome him. No one can tell how long it will take for a soul to leave the physical body, but to anyone who sees spirits, this is usually an indication that it won't take much longer. My sister, brother-in-law and I kept to our word and sat outside to have a last meal. Unfortunately it was too late in his life for him to sit with us. He was sleeping heavily in his room. Although he didn't open his eyes, he did give a slight nod that he had heard us. Because he was unable to eat with us was why we decided to eat outside; we didn't want the smell of food to disturb him. Whilst sitting outside, a yellow butterfly flew very slowly between us, stopping in the centre of the table. It had flown out of my uncle's room. My sister had seen it fly in there. Then we saw another. They danced around each other again in the centre of the table. I looked at my sister and said I thought it was a sign and the time may have come. We walked back into Uncle's room and only had enough time to tell him a huge thank you for all the good times and that we loved him as he took three deep breaths. On the final breath, I saw only what I can describe as a beautiful array of colours swirling out from him as his soul left his physical body. His soul had departed this life very gently, and we were so blessed to have been allowed to be with him. On the same day that he passed, each member of our family saw two yellow butterflies, hence the title for this book. This included one of my children, who usually has a fear of them but said the one she saw came right up to her and nearly settled on her, and she felt calm. I truly believe this was a sign from the spirit world as butterflies represent freedom and transformation.

CHAPTER 12

Grief

THIS CHAPTER IS included to help many of you who are experiencing or have experienced grief. It is in no part meant to be maudlin but instead to help you from a spiritual perspective on how it may be better to travel through and process. During the time Mum was in hospital, I could sense her dad around her in the spirit realm. I asked him to go away as none of us were ready to let her go yet. Mum asked several times if she was dying. "We hope not. Let them try the new antibiotics," we told her. You see, we knew how ill she was but were clinging on for her to recover. As a healer, I had many friends sending healing, and so was I. It is very difficult as a healer to be so close to someone so ill.

Accepting that it may be the person's pathway not to recover was very hard. Two days before her death, she told me she was so tired and had enough. I told her again just to wait and see. The next day she didn't open her eyes, but I played one of her favourite pieces of music to her, and she acknowledged it with a nod. As I left, I told her if it was her time, to pass gently. If it wasn't, that I would expect her to tell me off when she recovered! One of my sisters told her the same. I believe fully that we sense when someone is passing, and it is the spirit world's way to soften the loss. On this final day, I was aware that her mum had come to be with her. Usually at these times I sense the room filling up with relations from the spirit world to help the soul cross over. This time I was so blank. As it was my mum, I didn't want her to pass over yet. My connection to spirit felt like a void, and trying to reach Yin, one of my guides, felt impossible. When we are in grief, we shut out and close down so much from any form of reality or truth we know.

The day she passed, I woke early and looked at the clock. So did my sisters. We all knew that she was no longer with us in this world. This often happens to people when close family or friends die; it is an inner knowing. Sure enough, it was confirmed. Mum had passed in the early morning. When a soul is about to pass over, it sometimes lingers because the family is trying to keep the loved one here. I have seen many times when a family member has said he or she will see the person the next day. In my truth and experience, this can prolong the soul's passing. Souls need closure, to be wished well, told they are loved, and an actual goodbye said. This helps them to go to the light. My uncle waited until we were with him. My mum chose to pass on her own. She knew we wouldn't have coped being with her, and I was fully aware that her mum had come to help her.

Being a clairvoyant but still shocked by my loss, I was surprised to have immediate contact from her. A friend passed me a message from her too, and then another, quite specific. I feel that as I set her up in a healing space that was to help her leave this world if it was her time, she went quickly. Therefore, she was able to connect easily. My feelings during this phase were of utter grief and trauma accompanied by periods of calm. I even considered whether I had made her go as I had set up the healing space if needed. Yin soon cleared me of those feelings. In circle I said to my group that I thought Yin had left me. Instead, he channelled through that he was feeling my grief and loss. He was still with me, and because we are so close, he could feel my pain and felt it himself. He was just surrounding me with love and light. During those dark immediate days of grief, I felt a loving, protective energy around me. One friend told me that when she went to send me healing, she intuited not to. My guides had closed around me for total support. Everyone is well meaning at these times, but if, like I described in chapter 7, we are too open, we can attract all sorts of energies. All the thoughts and emotions that pass through your mind at the time. It is almost like losing grip on reality.

Despite having contact with Mum. I still wanted her on the earth plane. This is natural to feel and part of the grief. One day I was up and could function; another day I felt very low. The feelings then that I shouldn't grieve because I could sense her around and had the ability to be in contact with her. Also because of my healing practice, it felt bizarre to connect to feelings of disassociation with the spirit world. At times I doubted my guides, and my messages and dreams were quite sensational. None of them made sense, and there were moments of such vivid dreams that it felt like a parallel universe. I recalled saying to my mum in one of my dreams, "Oh, you are here. You didn't die after all. That was a bad dream. I am so glad I woke up." Of course the reality was that in fact I did then wake up and feel the emotion all over again. At these times I spent time meditating and shedding overwhelming tears. By doing the meditation, I calmed my mind and put in perspective the fact that grief is part of the human process. I recognised the need to put into practice what I suggested to others, to allow the ebb and flow of it. It has been an experience from my childhood when I preferred to cry inside, with the almost stiff upper lip. When it is someone close to you who passes, it actually doesn't make any difference how in control you wish to remain. The feelings will come out. It is therefore better to allow them; this does give some sense of control. Plus it has been a lesson for me that it is safe to release my pain. It has given others the chance to help me. I can remember years ago with Marguerite, one of my mentors. When I told her of my embarrassment when being given gifts, she told me that when I give to others, I feel good. She was right, I did. So Marguerite explained that the joy and pleasure I felt when giving, was also felt by the people who were giving to me. Those were some of the many wise words given to me, and I likened them to allowing others to help me through my grief. It is a strange feeling when you are a healer to feel so lost, but it is okay. The support of friends and family has been wonderful and forged different bonds between us.

When Mum first passed, I felt numb. Many say there can be anger, but that wasn't my experience. Although at first I felt it wasn't her time, it took me a while to accept it was. Her death was a shock to us all, and with all my spiritual beliefs, the concept of passing before her time didn't fit with me. Linking to Yin, he was able to show me that it was part of Mum's contract. As a family and piecing things together that Mum said, we are beginning to realise that she already knew; she had made provisions for many things. During the last month of her life, Mum was also speaking about when she would be gone. We kept laughing and saying not yet. It was peculiar looking back as at that time she was well and still active.

It is very difficult to understand that much of life is pre-planned. Many decisions we make before coming to the earth plane—the length of our lives, and what we chose to do. Now I would not say that all deaths are pre-planned or buy into the theories some hold that illness or disability are also chosen. That is a very different subject and holds many personal beliefs. It is an individual's way of looking at life and death, and at times, it has religious beliefs attached to it. My own are individual to me, so I can only share what I feel. When I miscarried a baby many years ago, I would never have wanted to believe that the child chose not to come at that time to the earth plane. In fact, I would have been very angry at anyone suggesting such a thing. As my spiritual development has increased, I now believe through communication with the soul of my child that she did decide for herself not to come then. The grief I experienced then, such a raw pain I never thought would heal, took years to lessen. The doctor was appalling and made me feel awful with the way I was told. This contributed to my sad feelings and likely the time it took to begin any form of healing. At the time of my loss, I was not very involved with spirit practice. It can only be a private journey for any type of grief, and my healing from the pain was finalised when I felt able to call my company after her. It was a name I had chosen for her when I was expecting her. Each year I still light a candle in her honour and now accept it wasn't her pathway to come to me at that time. If you have experienced loss like this, allow yourself to acknowledge it does take time. It also doesn't matter how many other people have gone through the same experience. Yours is unique, as are your feelings.

Over the years I have worked with many people through bereavements, and for some it is quick and looks to outsiders as though they could not have cared much. It is easy for others to judge when they are not in the same position. My nan taught me that in her experience, it is often the case that the harder someone grieves, the quicker they heal. This is why some widows remarry quickly. It isn't that they stopped loving their spouses or have forgotten them. It is just a desire of humans to be happy. Let's face it, this is what we chose an earthly life for. I have yet to meet anyone who genuinely wishes to be miserable. Our happiness is also the desire of spirit. I have never communicated with a spouse in spirit who has been angry or sad that his or her partner still this side is happy and getting on with life. They come through with messages of such love and pleasure and reassurances. In some of my readings to clients, the spirits have been very excited that they have met someone new to spend their lives with. This doesn't mean that we are constantly watched, but those in the spirit world are aware if loved ones are anxious about how they continue their lives without them. They will communicate through a medium or other spiritual channel to obtain reassurance. It is also how you feel intuitively; it will always be feelings of love and joy. All of us have the chance to still be reunited at the end of our lives with spirits who have gone before if that is the desire. The spirit world doesn't have the jealousy that humans do, so there will not be any recriminations. Other people may still feel the pain for many years after; some never fully recover. I have worked with people who feel guilt that they are still alive and then punish themselves for enjoying life. This is when I feel the love and compassion from the spirit world to communicate that they love seeing those left behind living fulfilling lives. Often when a person has a long-term illness, he or she passes on messages to others in the family to do things they weren't able to do during their lifetime. To me that indicates they want others to be successful and happy.

People mean well during times of bereavement. But with the intention of helping, they can sometimes get it wrong. I was fortunate when my mum passed as friends knew I would be private and speak to them and ask for help when I needed it. Therefore, use your intuition if someone around you is bereaved. It is something that can bring out the best and the worst in people as it is something that is often uncomfortable to discuss. Many people hedge around the subject or feel awkward or embarrassed. As healers we are taught how to help. It is the adage of being a good listener. Also realise that not everyone has the same thoughts or spiritual beliefs you may. Be sensitive to those feelings. I wouldn't expect my family or friends to feel how I do about my mum's passing. It would be ideal, but we don't live in an ideal world; we are all experiencing a human life. Like as a child when I freaked my sister out and loved scaring her, she may not be prepared to hear that I have contact with Mum. Although her beliefs are that Mum is still there, it is likely a different interpretation than what I sense.

Summary

You have the right to grieve despite how spiritually attuned you are. Others may help but may not understand how you are feeling or what to say.

Consider your thoughts whether people know when they are going to pass or if you feel it just happens. Think about religious impacts on death and the dying process.

Remember that bereavement, for some, doesn't have to be total despair. If you feel calm and at peace with death, that is fine. Everyone is unique, so their grieving will be. For some it is a release of pain or illness, so it may even be a cause for celebration. Don't judge others on how they come to terms with death, and don't be judged yourself.

Exercise

Use this exercise if you have been bereaved and are finding it hard to move forward through the trauma. Remember that there are many organisations to help with bereavement and, of course, help from your doctor will be available. Recognise if the grief is too much and seek help. Family and friends are good to be around as well.

You may wish to light a candle. As in previous exercises, make sure the space you are relaxing in is calm and energetically clear. Make certain you have the time to spend doing this and fully coming back to awareness before driving, working, or other activities.

Relax and focus on your breath coming in and out. Keep relaxing until you reach the point of nothing, just the in and out of your breath. Keep relaxing, and allow your awareness to come to your body. Note where you are holding tension and tightness related to the sadness. Notice how it feels. Does it have a colour, a shape, or something else. With the next few breaths, allow any tightness or shapes to relax and soften. Breath and watch the colours becoming brighter and your feelings becoming peaceful. Stay in this space for a while. At the end of the exercise, bring your awareness back to where you are. Clap your hands, move your feet, and get fully back in body. This is a space you can access as many times as you wish.

AFTERWORD

YOU HAVE READ many of my thoughts and beliefs throughout this book. You may have tried some of the exercises at the end of the chapters. Some you will have embraced, others felt uncomfortable with. I hope above all that you have enjoyed it as much as I have sharing my knowledge. During the reading of this book, you will find that I had turbulent times in life. All of those I got through with help and a strong sense and belief in spirit. Much of what I experienced was minor compared to losing my mum, particularly as I was close to finishing the book. That made it incredibly hard. I had kept my writing a secret as my desire was to give her my first copy. I know I will not be able to do that now. However, I do know that she will be aware of my work. With hindsight, we all have a wish to turn back time. So don't put off today what you can share. It may help another. Be kind, be generous, and love yourself.

Also during the time of writing this, late 2019 to early 2020, as a world we are experiencing the coronavirus pandemic. This has had so many justifiably worried. Many will survive this, and many souls sadly will pass over. Lots of people will not understand the whys or hows. Many people have different theories such as conspiracies set up by governments or countries. I have heard horror stories of how people from Asian countries have been treated abysmally. Anytime humanity scorns other humans we stop our development. No one can truly know where it came from or why, but the few who have taken it out on other countries are so misguided. Once again people with very little materially have been blamed. I say materially as we cannot measure people's wealth by their possessions. It has been for me as a healer very painful to see so much judgement of our fellow people from other countries. We all come from the same world; we just live in different parts of it. Our individual countries' cultures make us unique. In the West, many were disturbed by the East's way of treating animals. If that is their cultures and upbringing, are we really morally able to judge? Should we be looking at it from another perspective? I am quite sure there are things that other countries do that many across the globe find strange or as equally abhorrent. This spiritual journey teaches us not to judge, and when we begin it, it can be one of the hardest we endure.

When I have been meditating during this time, I have been aware of an energy coming forward. I asked who it was and as always, used my, "If not from the light, leave this space." He told me he was Enoch. I wondered why he was coming to me, and so I researched him. Enoch is mentioned in several places in the Bible. He was a prophet and foretold many things that would happen. Now I am not a biblical person, as mentioned in another chapter, but I do sit up and listen when I receive information to research from a prophet. If you choose to look him up, his story makes fascinating reading about thoughts on God, angels, and why he foretold the flood and other prophecies. As always, I keep an open, sceptical mind, but some of his words did sound true. I will deepen my understanding of the message, but for me it will be for personal use at this time. As an energy healer, I will not create the possibility of more fear, as the world mentioned by Enoch is ending and there will be a new beginning. Of course, having not researched enough, this could have referred to another time in the past. But it does seem strange to me that I should receive this prophet in meditation at this time. Metaphorically, we could say that the coronavirus is an ending of such and for many. Hopefully to be replaced with more thoughtfulness, understanding, and kindness.

There is a large network of energy healers set up who have been sending out regular healing for this. They, like me, often doubt their abilities. How can such a grim virus take over our world? I also consider the thought that healing can cause a healing crisis. Therefore, could all the healing that has been sent out be the reason the virus spread so rapidly? Not making it worse, but speeding up the delivery? The calm after the storm will come, and I am sure at the time this goes to print and you read it, we will all be living in a much different world.

The coronavirus was something I sensed back in December 2019. Like the visions I have had many times in the past, this was something I had an eerie feeling about at the time. I told my husband about something really big coming to completely change the world. I did not know at the time what it was. When Mum passed, I wondered if it was that; that certainly changed my world. However, this pandemic took over and the realisation of what I was tuning into changed. So you see, I cannot answer whether this was something that was meant to happen because I, amongst I am sure many others, had a knowing. Or was it possibly to make people stop and care for each other and their environment. At the start of it, many did the opposite and took more for themselves. Fear was everywhere, and there were concerns over running out of food. Eventually this began to ease, and volunteers came forward. My awful point came when I realised how lucky we are in the West to have thousands of ventilators. I read that one country only had one for a million people. That fell very flat with me. With hope and prayer, let us be able to respond and help those countries. Was this Mother Earth crying for all we have all taken as humans and our greed and lack of sharing with others? Was it that the sky was so full of our toxic airplane fumes that it now has to rest? The seas, too, are able to breathe, and the birds continue to sing. Whatever the reason for this, as part of the human race and as a spiritual person, I personally feel there were massive lessons to learn from this. Did we forget as humans to look after our elders, a painful lesson that so many will be taken from us? A spiritual journey is a wake-up call. When you start analysing and thinking, you have to consider without judgement all views, regardless of whether they are painful or happy. I send you all blessings and wish that you are able to move through the trauma that many of you will have faced.

May the light always shine with and on you. May you always have a guide by your side. May you know the wisdom to walk away or push through to triumph. May your spiritual journey be blessed and progressive. And even when you falter, may you feel strong enough to return to your pathway.

Namaste

GRATITUDE

TO MY MUM. Clearly without her encouragement, I truly would not be the person I am today. Albeit she did put up with me.

My sisters, Jane and Anne, who put up with so much. I was a trying sibling!

My children, they know who they are, I adore you all. All the pestering for grammar checks and punctuation, letting me share snippets of your lives. Without you all life would not have been so fun or trying. Thank you for coming into my life.

My grandson, who without his laugher and sunshine my life would be very different. A daily reminder in those huge eyes of what it is that makes us spiritual and feel unconditional love.

My husband, Kevin, for his support when I was flagging and numerous cups of tea, that later in the day turned into wine! And for allowing me to share his experience of painting with his guides.

Of course my close friends. I will not name you individually for fear of leaving some out, although I know you all. Your encouragement through my spiritual journey has been priceless, sincere thanks.

But to my best friend, Carol, we have travelled many a path and a lifetime together. If it were not for you, this book would still be in my head. The craters in the road, the tears, sweat, and pushing to write. The laughter, frustrations, wobbles, and encouragement. Much love to you, my friend. If we choose another lifetime, may we be best friends or family in it.

My guides, too, for their work enabled me to experience all this. Yin for his channelling, love, and correcting me, and helping when I was off my subject. And Akbar for acknowledging right from wrong.

Not forgetting my fur babies, Abraham and Mitsi. Abraham for his incessant purring and affection, including walking on my keyboard, reminding me to save my work. I would have needed a lot of retyping without you! Mitsi for your cuteness and watching all the spirits in our home, showing me you experience the spirit world too.

For all of you who will read and I sincerely hope learn from and enjoy this book, the journey is tough, but the treasure is worth it.

Much love and gratitude
Caroline

ABOUT THE AUTHOR

CAROLINE MALONE IS a spiritual teacher, energy healer, channel, and mentor. Since childhood, she has communicated and worked with spirits. As an adult, she has written and run workshops and circle for many years, teaching and encouraging people on their spiritual journeys. Throughout her spiritual life, Caroline has been a channel for spirits and been given a new healing modality called Paradigm Healing© that the spirit world wishes her to share and teach. She believes that love, gratitude, and kindness are the ways to live true to ourselves. Caroline's guides have worked with her for many years and have encouraged and helped her development. She wishes to acknowledge them as part of her as an author.

www.CarolineMalone.co.uk
www.TwoYellowButterflies.com

Printed in Great Britain
by Amazon